To Marty + Dave Leavenworth
with best regards.

Preston Dillon
May 23, 1999

LIABILITY

Preston Dilts, M.D.

VANTAGE PRESS
New York

To Mary

Published by Vantage Press, Inc.
516 West 34th Street, New York, New York 10001

Manufactured in the United States of America
ISBN: 0-533-12875-7

Library of Congress Catalog Card No.: 98-90665

0 9 8 7 6 5 4 3 2 1

The first thing we do, let's kill all the lawyers.

—*Shakespeare: Henry the Sixth, Part II*

Acknowledgment

This novel could not have been written without the advice and support of a number of people. Many thanks to Jim, Warren, Kathe, Cynthia, and Nancy. Most important has been the continuing love, support, and valued criticism by Mary, my wife.

1

Janet reached for the telephone.

"Hello, Mrs. Smith. What's up?"

"My water broke about three o'clock.," Angie said excitedly, "and I'm having contractions."

"How close together are they?"

"About five minutes."

"Why don't you go on to Memorial Hospital. I'll meet you there."

"Okay, but hurry."

Janet Jankowski rushed through her last patient, signed some charts and dictation, and talked with Nancy, her nurse.

"It's good to get the Smith delivery over with, because then I won't have anyone due for over two weeks. These last three weeks have been murder. I haven't had a full night's sleep for the whole time."

"You do look tired," Nancy answered. "I hope she delivers quickly so you can get home at a reasonable hour tonight."

"Thanks. I'll see you tomorrow."

A few minutes after six o'clock, Janet wearily left the office and headed for the hospital. She met Angie and Bill Smith in labor and delivery and congratulated Angie; she was in early labor, about three out of ten centimeters dilated, and her cervix was completely thinned out.

"The baby's head is well down in your pelvis, so things are moving along really nicely. I'll get the anesthesiologist going on the epidural right now, so we'll be all set when you need it."

"I'm ready now," Angie cried out. "This really hurts."

"Soon. Soon," Janet soothed her.

An external fetal heart monitor and contraction gauge were strapped to her abdomen so all could listen and watch. The anesthesiologist inserted the epidural catheter without difficulty, and an hour after admission, when she was five centimeters dilated, they injected a local anesthetic to relieve Angie's discomfort. Then an internal contraction monitor was inserted and a fetal scalp electrode was attached, requiring Angie to remain in bed.

Bill sat with Angie, holding her hand; they were both fixated on the monitor screen and the beeping.

Janet was in and out but always close by.

"You're beautiful, darling," Bill whispered. "I love you very much. I hope it won't be long before he's here." Since Bill planned to be with her for the delivery, he had already changed into a scrub suit, shoe covers, cap, and mask.

Angie smiled at him as he wiped her face with a cold washcloth. The epidural had a marked calming effect, but her contractions continued without interruption every four minutes.

At six centimeters dilation, two hours after admission, the fetal heart-rate monitor showed a two-and-a-half-minute dip to eighty beats per minute during and after a contraction. Angie, Bill, and Janet collectively breathed a sigh of relief when it came back up to normal, about one hundred forty per minute. There wasn't much variation in the heart-rate rhythm between contractions, and in fact, there hadn't been much since the monitor was put on at admission.

Janet was at her bedside when it happened, and she and the nurses quickly turned Angie over to her left side, put an oxygen tube in her nose, and increased the flow rate of the IV. The next contraction caused a brief acceleration in the heart rate, followed by a minor dip, which lasted forty-five seconds.

"Doctor, what's going on? Is my baby okay?" Angie was clearly frightened.

Bill tried his best to be supportive, but he, too, was obviously alarmed.

"We don't know what this means yet," Janet carefully explained, "except that I don't think it's dangerous. The lack of beat to beat variability is a little odd—"

"Doctor, please explain that so I can understand," Bill interrupted.

"A baby's heart usually has some variation in rate, by a few beats per minute, unlike ours. The rate may flatten out with pain medicines or sleep," Janet tried to explain. "We call it beat-to-beat variability."

Bill and Angie's faces mirrored their lack of understanding.

"But this one dip, by itself," Janet rushed on, "isn't enough to change our plans, especially with the acceleration before the next contraction, which is really reassuring. That dip with the next one is quite normal; it only went down fifteen beats per minute. Decelerations like that happen with most contractions in the last half of labor, especially when the baby's head is down in the pelvis like yours is. We'll watch very closely. If there's a repeat drop like this first one, we may have to do a cesarean section. Just to be prepared, we'll get everything set up, so we can do it in a hurry if it's necessary."

"Just try to make sure the incision's down low, if you can, where it won't show," Bill blurted out.

"We'll agree to anything to make sure my baby is okay," Angie interrupted. "Why are you waiting to do a c-section?" she demanded to know.

"We really don't have any reason to do one right now," Janet answered quickly. "One of the maternal-fetal specialists happened to be out at the desk while this happened, and he looked at the pattern on the TV monitor. He agrees with me that there's no reason to do a c-section right away. We'll be ready for one if we need to, but we should continue watching for now."

"Okay, but we don't want to take any chances," urged Angie.

"Darling, I'm sure everything will be okay. Dr. Jankowski is right here if anything happens." Bill tried to calm her, as Janet stepped out briefly.

"Bill, I'm scared," Angie wailed.

The fetal heart-rate pattern was reassuring for the next thirty minutes. Janet sat with Angie, examined her, and reported that she was seven centimeters dilated. While she was talking to them about the delivery, another dip occurred, down to sixty beats per minute. This one persisted for three minutes after the contraction was over.

"Oh, my God! My baby's in trouble! Doctor, do something!" shouted Angie, as soon as it was clear that the heart rate was not coming back up when the contraction ended.

"We're going to do a cesarean section right now," Janet yelled to the nurses. She disconnected the monitors and started moving the bed to the door. "Let's get going." Janet bent over Angie's head as she pushed the bed. "We may have to put you to sleep with general anesthesia, because the epidural isn't high enough for the c-section, and it takes longer to get it up than to do a general."

"Anything. Just make sure that my baby is okay." Angie was the picture of torment. Her eyes were wide, her face ashen, her jaw sagging, her breathing ragged, and her voice shrieking.

Janet raced down the hall with the bed. She had to brake hard to make the turn through the OR door. The nurse finally caught up with her as she maneuvered the bed next to the OR table.

"Where's anesthesia? I need them right now," Janet yelled. "Quick, help me lift her to the table. That's the way. You put in the catheter while I get into my gown and gloves," she ordered the nurse. "Somebody hook up the monitor. I won't take time to scrub. Where's the resident?" she yelled to the OR staff. The anesthesia team ran through the door. Janet explained everything to them as they strapped Angie down.

The heart tones came back up to ninety beats per minute, which was somewhat encouraging to Janet but unnoticed by Bill or Angie, as the nurse put in the bladder catheter and scrubbed Angie's belly with antibacterial soap.

The anesthesia team, then up to speed, quickly put Angie to sleep by inserting a tube into her windpipe. They hurried so fast that the paralyzing agent, succinylcholine, wasn't fully in effect when they inserted the tube.

Angie bucked a couple of times, kept on the table by the straps. Janet saw that her eyes were open, and for a moment, she feared Angie would remember the tube. Just as quickly, Janet realized that the fast-acting barbiturate used to put Angie to sleep before anything was done would induce amnesia.

"Come on! Let's go! Here, help me drape," she demanded of the scrub tech. "Get the resident."

Bill watched in seeming horror as Janet quickly draped Angie's abdomen and rapidly made a midline incision from her umbilicus to her pubic bone.

"Get your hands out of the way," she elbowed the resident who had just come in, whispering hoarsely. "Go around to the other side. You can help better there."

She continued the incision through the other layers with a second stroke of the knife, exposing the uterus. She and the resident incised the bladder flap, pushed it down, and entered the uterus.

"That's the way. We're almost there."

Ninety seconds after starting the incision and three minutes after the sleep agent was injected, Janet delivered a seven-pound twelve-ounce boy with a barely adequate heart beat and a shrill cry. While he breathed on his own, he was limp and hung like a rag doll.

"Damn, this baby's floppy," she muttered to the resident.

As she handed the baby to the neonatologist, Janet turned to Bill to find him sitting on a stool, holding his head in anguish, looking green. *Oh, damn*, she thought. *I wish he weren't here.*

Bill jumped up to go to the bassinet to watch the resuscitation.

"What's the matter, doctor? What's going on? Why isn't he crying more? Why doesn't he move?" He danced around behind the pediatric team to get a better look and had to be asked, several times, to stay out of the way. When they rushed the baby to the Memorial Neonatal Intensive Care Unit, he followed along.

"We don't know right now. It shouldn't be serious, since his breathing and heart rate seemed to respond right away to suction and stimulation. He'll go to our NICU here for observation, and I'm sure they'll get the neonatologists from the University Hospital to take a look. Everything should be okay," Janet tried to answer before he ran out.

"Sorry I yelled, everybody," Janet apologized as soon as Bill was gone. "I don't like to do that, but this was so unexpected, I had to get us moving as fast as possible."

While she was closing the uterus and abdomen, Janet reviewed her management with the resident and could not explain what had happened. There had not been any bleeding, and the umbilical cord had not been around the baby's neck or knotted. There wasn't any meconium in the amniotic fluid. The placenta hadn't separated prematurely or looked abnormal. Nothing untoward had happened with the anesthesia during labor or the cesarean. The maternal-fetal specialists had agreed with all of her management. However, the baby's Apgar scores were two at one minute and four at five minutes. So, she worried that she missed something.

"Be sure to send the placenta to pathology. Maybe they can find something to explain this." She really didn't have much hope it would help, but she wanted to cover all the bases.

As soon as she was finished, Janet went to the NICU to check on the baby. The ten-minute Apgar score was five. There had been no change—he was floppy and had a weak, shrill cry.

One of the University's neonatologists was there, but she had nothing further to suggest. In fact, she was rather pessimistic. Janet took Bill back to the recovery room to see Angie.

"Your son should be okay, Mr. Smith. These things happen occasionally, and almost always the baby turns out to be perfectly normal. Please help me reassure Mrs. Smith. We need her up and around as quickly as possible, so she will recover and be able to take care of him." Janet didn't feel as upbeat as she tried to sound.

"I will," Bill answered despairingly.

Angie was awake, but not very alert, because of the anesthesia. Janet tried to reassure her, but she doubted that Angie would remember much until morning, when she hoped to be able to explain the whole thing to them.

"Stay here with Mrs. Smith for now. The neonatologists will let you know if anything happens. Your wife will need you when she wakes up from the anesthesia."

"I will," Bill responded.

Janet left Bill there and went to the desk to dictate the operative report, write orders, and complete the chart.

Back in the recovery room, Bill sat with his head in his hands, looking forlornly at Angie who alternated between groggy moans and sleep. She was to be moved to her room in a couple of hours.

Janet swung by the NICU to check on the baby: no change. She trudged to the dressing room, emotionally drained, where she tossed her sweat-soaked scrub shirt and pants into a hamper, annoyed that they clung to her plump figure. *Even the large size is getting too tight*, she thought. *Damn*. She considered a shower and decided it was too late; she was too exhausted to do even that. Instead, she pulled on her slip and dress, and as she looked in the mirror to brush her short, but thick, dark hair into place, she frowned. It was matted and wet, framing her round face. *At least the gray doesn't show*, she thought.

While brushing her teeth to get rid of the awful taste in her mouth, she decided to leave her hair for the morning, even though it meant getting up earlier. Then she headed for the doctor's parking lot. *Well, that's the last one for a while*, she reflected wearily. *I've got to get some sleep.*

She drove very carefully through a light drizzle. She was chilled to the bone; she had forgotten her coat, and her wet underwear made her situation even worse. The drive home to Webster Groves took twenty-five minutes. Finally, she pulled into the garage, almost unconscious with fatigue.

She walked through her colonial country kitchen, nuzzled by Jenny, a black Lab, who bounded across the room. "At least she's up to welcome me," Janet groused to herself as she left her briefcase, stuffed with medical journals, in the study, wondering why she bothered to carry them around at all. She never had time to look at them anymore.

She looked around the desk, saw nothing that Mike, her husband, had marked as urgent in the pile of mail, turned off the lights, and headed for bed. She had to drag herself up the stairs, pleased someone had left a light on for her. Two nights ago, she had almost fallen flat, tripping over one of the children's backpacks at the foot of the stairs. Now there were night lights in the hall and on the stairs, which made the house a little less cold in the lonely hours of the night.

Mike was already asleep and didn't awaken beyond a mumbled goodnight. She lay there in the dark for a long time, going over and over everything that had happened, still worried that she had missed something. She could not imagine what caused the baby to be so floppy and to respond so poorly. Nothing like this had ever happened to her before. Janet was restless all night and had to push herself to get going in the morning. She was so late that she didn't have a chance to talk with Mike or the kids at all.

The air was crisp and cool, and there was little trace of rain remaining. The long drive seemed shorter after a few hours sleep, and she rushed in to begin a typical day. She had five obstetrics and three postsurgery gynecology patients to see, so rounds took more than an hour and a half. She spent as much time with each of them as they desired, sending home three of the OBs and one of the GYN postops. The other two OBs, including Angie, had had cesarean sections. Discharge instructions and record-keeping were time-consuming and tedious. She skipped going to the OB lounge and didn't stop to say more than a passing hello to any of the other doctors she saw.

2

"Mr. and Mrs. Smith, we don't know exactly what's going on with your son, but we do know that he's not responding the way we'd like him to. We think he should probably be transferred to the NICU at the university for care and work up," suggested Dr. George Thomas, the University neonatologist who took over the baby's care when he saw him very early the morning after the delivery, before Janet made rounds. "We'll decide over the next twenty-four hours, but you should start planning for the move now." Thomas stood at attention, halfway between the door and bed.

"Please, tell us what's wrong? Why doesn't he respond?"

"As I said, we don't know for sure," Thomas pontificated. "However, it looks very much like your son's developing cerebral palsy. We think we can make a more certain diagnosis and offer better treatment with the facilities we have in the NICU at University Hospital."

"Oh, God, Bill. This can't be. How could this happen, doctor?" Angie was startled, fully awake.

"Mrs. Smith, it would appear that whatever is going on with him now is related to your labor and delivery. We don't know for sure, and may never know, but that's our operating theory for now."

"What are you saying? Do you mean that they didn't respond quickly enough?" Bill demanded to know.

"That very well could be. I think that an earlier cesarean section might have prevented these problems," Thomas spoke slowly, but very confidently. "In fact, I'm quite sure of it. We'll know more with time. For right now, we may need to move your son. You'll have to sign some papers. Is that okay?"

"Yes, of course. I'll be going home tomorrow or the next day. I assume we can come see him?" Angie asked.

"We encourage you to visit as frequently as you can. I'll stop by again this evening." Thomas went from their room to the post-partum desk and the chart carousel. He turned it slowly to Angie's, carried the chart to the counter, and opened it. After a moment's hesitation, he wrote a long note in Angie's record, detailing his opinion about Janet's management and the effect it had on the baby. Then he repeated the same statement in the baby's record in the NICU.

When Janet came by later, she found Angie doing very well physically, but both she and Bill were quite distant. She couldn't understand their complete lack of questions. Janet expressed her uncertainty about the baby and went to the desk to write a note in the chart.

Thomas's page-long accusation was obviously upsetting to Janet. She entered a note countering his, referring to her dictated operative report, which laid out her differing opinions. She left the hospital even more worried.

Janet drove to her office, which was ten blocks away. The ten-year-old brick building with two floors was on the edge of a residential neighborhood. Janet rented two-thirds of the first floor; the other one-third was occupied by the owner, an accountant. The second floor was split between two lawyers.

Janet's office was comfortable and feminine. The waiting and reception areas were done in pastels and flower prints. There were also several plants and ferns and stacks of women's magazines by the cozy white wicker furniture.

When Janet arrived, just after nine-thirty, Nancy informed

her that three return GYN patients were already in exam rooms and that a new GYN patient was in her consultation room.

I'm behind before I even get started, she thought.

"Dr. Jankowski, you look tired. Did Mrs. Smith keep you up last night?"

"Yes, she delivered after nine o'clock, so I got home late. We had to do a cesarean, and the baby's not doing very well. I don't know why. I really am tired. What else do we have today?" She hung her coat behind the door to her consultation room.

"There are already a couple of phone calls, which I arranged for you to return around noon, and there are eleven more patients scheduled this morning and twenty-five this afternoon because of rescheduling. These daytime deliveries ruin our schedule. I put the rest of yesterday's dictation on your desk to be signed. Here are the telephone notes."

Janet stuck them on the corner of her blotter.

"I sure hope I don't have any interruptions today, because I need to get home to spend time with Mike and the kids," she said wearily. "If you don't mind, ask Darlene to call the patients scheduled from three-thirty on to see if they can come in at noon or earlier. If they can't, reschedule them tomorrow. I'd like to finish by four if we can. You two can leave early too, or at least on time for a change. I'll squeeze in the phone calls." Janet parked her briefcase and looked longingly at her chair. *I can't. I'll fall asleep*, she thought.

"Doctor, you know I'll do anything you want me to do. I don't think Darlene will mind either. But we worry about you. You need a rest, and this sure isn't a very good way to get one."

"Nancy, I know it. We'll have to do something soon to get things in control. If you have any ideas, I'd like to hear them. Ask Darlene, too."

"I will. Start in room one, and then go to the new patient. She says she has fibroids and wants to be scheduled for surgery.

We'll get through this day in a whiz."

"Nancy, you're the best." *I used to be able to keep up by myself,* she thought. *Now I'm almost totally dependent on Nancy.*

Janet's day in the office was hectic enough that she was immersed there, almost forgetting Angie, until she made rounds late in the day.

Meanwhile, Angie and Bill tried to cheer each other up. He even took her to the NICU in a wheelchair right after breakfast. The visit, however, was not reassuring. The baby had tubes in him for the IV and for breathing. Worst of all, he didn't move once.

"Oh, Bill! What are we going to do?" she wailed, when they went back to her room.

"Honey, I just don't know. Maybe Dr. Thomas is wrong, and maybe he'll be okay. He isn't even twenty-four hours old yet, so there's still time."

"I hope so," she cried, her voice still hoarse from the tube in her throat for the anesthesia.

They spent most of the day repeating the same questions. A second visit to the NICU in the midafternoon didn't provide answers, though, because there was no change.

Late that afternoon, the gulf between Janet and the Smiths was, if possible, wider. They were almost hostile in their attitude, answering questions only when forced and definitely not encouraging any other conversation. Janet had visited the nursery and couldn't report any improvement either. She suspected that Thomas has already been by to see them again, even though he hadn't added another note to the chart.

Janet did make it home by five-fifteen to be with the kids, who had surprisingly come home on time. They played video games, which Janet lost as usual, and talked about school. Neither Carol nor Michael would say anything about school or their report cards, so Janet decided to add that to the agenda for her talk with Mike. She was upset by her loss of closeness with her children. *I've got to spend more time with them*, she resolved.

Both Carol and Michael were tall and thin, like their father, and they both had his blond hair and blue eyes. They were full of energy and, most of the time, were good friends. Until they were left with the nannies almost constantly, they had been top performers in school and pretty good athletes.

Mike came home soon after five-thirty, hugged the kids, who scampered to meet him, kissed Janet quickly, and suggested that the two of them go to their favorite restaurant, Garibaldi's, where they could relax. Janet eagerly accepted.

"Let me ride with you instead of taking two cars. I arranged coverage for the evening, so I won't be called, and I don't want to drive anywhere tonight unless I have to. I'm too darn tired."

"Sure. Let's go right now, so we can get home early and put you to bed."

Mike parked near the entrance, and they were seated right away. The warmth inside and a pervasive but pleasant garlic smell engulfed them. The restaurant had a mixture of booths and tables in several rooms, on three levels, so privacy was encouraged. Each table had a white linen tablecloth and a fat wine bottle candlestick covered in wax. Hot bread, olive oil, and seasonings were brought immediately with their menus and a description of the specials.

"Hi, docs. How are you two this evening?" asked the owner.

"Hello, Vince. We're fine," Mike answered.

"You've got to relax sometime. You know what I mean?" Vince asked.

"Keep saying it, Vince. She needs to hear it from someone besides me," Mike urged him.

"Gotta go. Nice to see you."

Janet pushed the bread and candle aside, leaned across the

table, and took Mike's hands in both of hers.

"He's right, we don't go out enough. We can certainly afford it, and I think both of us could use more entertainment. We haven't been to a symphony or to a ballet for at least six months. We never go to jazz concerts anymore, either. And we never entertain at our house."

"I know," Mike replied.

"It's worse than that," she continued. "We used to have those tickets to the Cardinals so we could take the kids. That didn't work out, and now we don't go to anything. We don't seem to have any close friends to do things with. We've spent all our time practicing medicine, especially me, instead of getting involved in a church or country club or something else. I haven't talked to Kim in months. We really do need to make some changes."

"I know, honey, but I think you need to make most of the changes. I have my practice under pretty good control, so I can be home with you and the kids."

The waitress interrupted, so they both ordered the special, grilled sea bass, and a caesar salad to split.

"I know I've said this before, but you could stop doing obstetrics and limit your practice to gynecology," Mike continued. "Nights would be much easier then, and maybe your fatigue and irritability would disappear. Besides, we haven't made love in a long time. You're either at the hospital or too tired."

"I'm sorry. I miss you, too. That's easy enough to fix. I'll just make the time. But I don't understand what you mean by irritability."

"Well, lately, your temper has been a little short, and that's not like you at all. When you're upset, you usually eat more. The only thing I can assume is that some of the stuff I've heard about OB must be getting to you. Either that or you're working too hard. Maybe both. Think about it, please."

"What do you mean? I like delivering babies," Janet scowled.

"You know. Managed care and liability. That's the constant talk in the doctor's lounge at Memorial, at least when I'm there."

Their salads came. Both tried to eat and talk at once.

"Mike, you're right, of course. But you know, I've never had any problem with patients leaving my practice because of their insurance or for any other reason. I accept all the plans available at Memorial just to avoid any difficulties, and I spend a great deal of time talking with each of the patients and their husbands," she said, smiling.

"If you're not worried about something, then you must be working too hard. You're worn out all the time, and you snap at all of us."

"Thanks a lot. I guess this is beat-up-on-Janet night. Let's just stop, if you don't mind," she flared at him.

"Okay. Okay."

When their dinners came, they picked at their plates.

"I couldn't get much out of the kids about school either, especially Carol. I guess one of us needs to meet with their teachers," Mike began.

"I'll do it," she quickly answered.

"How? You don't have time for anything now."

"I'm going to take off Wednesday afternoons again, starting next week." She felt good about taking control and making a decision about her practice.

"That's nice. That will give you some time to rest as well."

She finally told him about the Smith delivery.

"I'm sorry to hear that. That's kind of like the last straw, on top of everything else. I'm sure it will work out."

"Thanks. I sure hope so."

Their conversation lagged a little.

"Listen, I wasn't trying to start a fight earlier," Mike said. "I wanted just the opposite—a nice, quiet evening out. I'm sorry. But something does have you out of sorts, and I can't see that it's anything the kids or I have done, so it must be your practice. Think about it, please."

She reached for his hand again.

"I guess you're right. All these nights in a row without enough sleep are just too much."

"The Boston Pops will be here a week from Saturday. I already got tickets. I hope that's okay?" Mike asked.

"Yes, I'd love to go. I'm sure I can get someone to cover. What a nice surprise."

"I want us to spend more time together, honey." Mike paused. "Are you finished?"

"Yes. It's good, but I'm just not hungry. Let's get the check. The kids should be going to bed by the time we get home," she said, still holding his hand and smiling invitingly at him.

Janet fell asleep in the car, awakening as they pulled into the garage.

Jenny welcomed them, banging the cooking island with her tail. The children were in their rooms, so Janet and Mike went to each to say good night and then went to their own bedroom.

Janet reached for Mike and pulled him down to her to kiss him. "Let's make love," she whispered. "I'll bet you can keep me awake that long."

"I'm sorry I picked on you tonight, and I will think of something to keep you awake," he answered, hugging her tightly and lifting her off her toes.

The next morning, Janet told Nancy to clear Wednesday afternoons and to schedule visits for the following week. She called her best friend, Kim Workman, and left a message inviting her to have lunch on Wednesday the next week. Then she dived into the office, full of patients, many of them rescheduled.

The baby began to have seizures that morning, at thirty-six

hours of age. His heart and lungs continued to function reasonably well, but he remained limp from medication, except during a seizure, and did not develop more than the faint, shrill cry. Late that morning, the Memorial pediatricians agreed with Thomas that the baby would be better off in the University Hospital NICU. In addition to better equipped facilities, they could do a more thorough work up there to find out the source of the problem or problems.

Janet was really disturbed by the Smith baby, knowing that she, too, would be shattered if anything had happened to one of her own children. She had talked about it with Mike at breakfast that morning.

"Janet, it's probably normal for them to be distant, with all the turmoil in their lives over this baby. I wouldn't read anything into it yet, even though Thomas hasn't helped any."

"I'm trying not to, but it isn't working."

Janet tried to be warm and friendly to the Smiths, without success, and was more alarmed by their now open hostility, which was aggravated by the news of the seizures. Thomas didn't write anything more in Angie's chart and, worse, he made no attempt to talk to Janet even though she tried to call him both days Angie was in the hospital.

3

Angie recovered very quickly from the cesarean section and went home on the third day, twenty-four hours after the baby was moved. They stopped at the University Hospital NICU to see Will, short for William N. Smith, Jr. There was no change from the day before. The seizures were rare and much less severe because of medication, but his general condition was the same.

Will was in a high-tech crib, with a plastic cover, which was used to look through and to help maintain temperature and humidity. An IV was dripping into a vein in his umbilical cord, and he had a mask over his face to provide oxygen. The IV was going to be switched to a vein in his scalp that afternoon. His eyes were closed and, again, he didn't move the entire time his parents watched.

The nurse told Angie and Bill that they could put gloves on and touch him through holes in the side of the crib, but both declined. They were too scared to even think of it.

Angie and Bill's trip home was somber, each too disturbed to know how to begin any type of conversation. Neighbors and friends had planned to be there to welcome them, but Bill had cancelled that; neither of them could handle the company. He asked them to come back over the next few days, one or two couples at a time, which they did.

Angie cried most of the time for the first day or two.

The live-in nurse, who was supposed to help with Angie and the baby until a nanny could be hired, did her best to get Angie settled.

"Honey, just you sit there and let me get everything for you. I'm assuming you want me to stay here for now, even though the baby isn't home yet. That's okay with me, as long as you want me."

Angie quickly agreed. Bill was uncertain, since they already had both a maid and a cook, but he wanted to help Angie in any way he could, so he concurred.

Wilma James was a registered nurse who worked exclusively as a live-in nurse with cancer patients, with people recovering from surgery or illness, and with new mothers. She was a fifty-four-year-old divorced woman with two children who were grown and gone. Her social life revolved entirely around her patients and their families. She was quite plump but attractive. She wore a white uniform, pants and smock.

Wilma was never still, either physically or verbally. She sat or stood closely when she talked with someone, always rocking side to side or front to back. Her eyes darted around taking in everything within view, without actually turning her head. Her hands moved incessantly to her hair, her necklace, her pockets, and back again. In short, she was a fidget. She also had an inquiring mind, the type usually called nosey. Angie and Bill were so engrossed with their own problems that they didn't notice at first.

Wilma loved to talk, and that probably helped the Smiths more than anything, especially Angie in her first few days at home. In their grief, Angie and Bill didn't know how to talk with each other and were very awkward with friends who came by.

Angie would ask repeatedly, "Bill, what are we going to do?"

"I don't know," he answered each time. "I still can't believe this has happened, especially when you had such a normal pregnancy. It's even harder to believe that he may never get better. Someone must have done something wrong. I need help. We need help. And I don't know where to get it. I don't even know where to start."

"Oh, honey, I'm so frightened and hurt by this that I seem to live minute by minute. I can't imagine this afternoon, let alone tomorrow or next week." She leaned against him.

"I know, darling. I'm the same way. It's absolutely devastating." He held her in his arms, careful not to push against her incision.

"I've always heard that c-sections were a piece of cake. Instead, I'm wiped out, and this incision hurts like crazy."

"Angie, you just had a major operation. I watched, and I know this had to be a lot tougher than a normal delivery, no matter what anybody says. Not being able to bring Will home just makes it worse."

Wilma interrupted them.

"Honey, are you ready for your shower? Here, let me help you up the stairs."

Bill was left alone in the family room, where he idly turned on the TV to a golf game. When Angie returned, ninety minutes later, they resumed staring at each other. That night, Bill held her while she fell asleep, crying.

Angie and Bill went to see Will twice every day, but that made them more distraught. They spent only a few minutes with him and more time with the nurses and residents hoping for reassurance, which was not forthcoming. Each evening, they talked some about the baby and themselves, but most of the time, they just stared into space.

A week after Angie came home, when Bill was sure she was recovering well from the surgery, he decided to go back to work, saying he'd take more time off when the baby came home.

"Bill, what are we going to do if he doesn't get better?"

"Darling, I don't know, but they haven't said it's hopeless yet. I tried to get some answers when we were there. It's like they were hiding something."

"I know. I heard some of it. This is nerve-racking, just waiting."

"I know. Honey, I'm going to start back at the office now. I can be home, or wherever you need me to be, very quickly. I won't schedule anything out of town for a while. You're strong enough to get around by yourself."

"Okay, dear. Wilma's here to keep me company."

After Bill returned to work, Angie and Wilma were soon talking about their families, their dreams, and their disappointments. Angie's dependence on Wilma grew quickly, while the maid and the cook took care of the rest of the house. She didn't regain her former vitality or vigor, and she even neglected her hair and makeup. When Angie wore the same skirt and blouse for three days in a row, Wilma intervened by laying out a fresh outfit for her daily, helping her dress, and brushing her hair.

While Bill was at work, Wilma began driving Angie to see Will twice a day. Each time, Will was still, except for small movements of his chest. The IV was removed from his scalp and a new tube was put in through his nose into his stomach to feed him. Otherwise, nothing changed.

Angie did touch Will after a while. The day came when her touch appeared to have caused him to have a seizure; she never tried again. Since he didn't learn to suck at all, she stopped pumping her breasts to take in the milk, even though the NICU nurses urged her to continue.

Several days after Bill returned to work, Angie asked him to meet her at the NICU.

"Honey, I'm full up today, and besides, I just can't look at him. He almost doesn't seem human with that tube, and he doesn't respond at all. I'm sorry, but I just can't go today." He couldn't seem to look her in the eye.

"Well, I'll keep going twice a day. We have to try," Angie pouted.

"I'll try, too," Bill answered, but he rarely found the time during the day, and neither of them wanted to go in the evening.

Bill was very busy at the office after ten days off and found himself dependent on work to avoid thinking about the problems at home. He began to get take-out food in the evening at the office, and he arranged business dinners after Angie started eating supper early with Wilma.

"Angie, what did you decide about your appointment with Dr. Jankowski today?" Bill asked a few days later. "Didn't she say she wanted to see you to check the incision at two weeks?"

"Yes, she did, but I just can't face her right now. I'm doing fine, so I called and told the nurse. She said it was okay."

"Do you have any more appointments with her?"

"I'm supposed to go at six weeks. I told her nurse I'd call to make an appointment."

"Let's not forget. I want to be sure you're okay, Angie. Please."

"Thanks, honey. I won't forget," but she didn't follow through.

"Mrs. Smith, you seem like an ideal couple. It's sure too bad something like this had to happen to such nice people like you," Wilma announced one evening two and a half weeks after the baby was born. "It sort of reminds me of another family I took care of a couple of years ago. She'd had surgery, and I came in to take care of her and the kids. She did poorly and had to go back into the hospital for tests. They found a sponge in her belly those doctors had left behind, and she had to have another operation to get it out. I always wonder if the doctors do it right."

"Wilma, are you suggesting that something was done wrong?"

"Well, I don't know, but you told me that the neonatologist suggested something went wrong during the delivery, that the delay in doing the c-section may have been responsible for your son's problems. I'd sure want to think about it some."

"What should we do? I don't know anything about this sort of thing." She looked bewildered.

"Probably nothing for right now. I suppose you should wait and see how things develop. Maybe he'll improve. It's just something to think about."

That night Angie talked to Bill about it.

"Wilma said something today that bothered me." She quickly related their conversation.

"Darling, we were right there. I don't know about this, about saying that something was done wrong." Bill looked confused.

"Honey, don't you remember the neonatologist, Dr. Thomas, and his comments to us the first time he saw us?"

"Yes, but let's think about it. I suppose you could ask Wilma about what to do." He didn't seem very enthusiastic.

"I'll do that," she snapped. "By the way, why are you coming home so much later than you used to? You rarely even eat here anymore."

"Sweetheart, that's not fair. Don't be upset with me, please. The truth is that I don't like being with Wilma. I know she's a big help with you, but her constant talking gets on my nerves. Also, I'm trying to catch up with work and to get a little ahead, if I can. It looks like we'll have some pretty heavy expenses for the baby and the nurses," he answered.

"That's another thing. Why don't you ever call the baby Will? He's named after you. In fact, you don't talk about him at all."

"Angie, I don't know," he groaned. "I guess I just haven't felt any attachment to him; I've never even been able to hold him." They held each other for a while, both close to tears.

"Oh, Bill. What are we going to do? This is tearing us apart."

"I've been trying to drown myself with work, and it's not doing any good. I think about him, about us, all the time, so it takes me longer to get things done. I can't even go out selling unless I'm forced to. Thank God we've got good salespeople who can pick up the slack."

"That's all Wilma and I talk about, Will and his problems. I've thought about letting her go, but then I'd be alone staring at the walls or TV, and that's worse. I wish you could be here, but I know you can't be."

"Honey, I think you should talk to Wilma about the lawyers. Maybe that will help."

"I will, first thing tomorrow."

In the morning, Wilma was more than helpful.

"Well, the last folks I told you about used a lawyer named Herbert Kline. He's in a firm called Kline and Jones. They specialize in this sort of thing, I think. I'm sure you can find their number in the phone book."

"Thanks, Wilma. Maybe I will call."

4

The Smith delivery became an unrelenting nightmare for Janet. She spent most of her waking hours agonizing about everything she had done and looking for ways she could have changed the result. She repeatedly showed the fetal heart-rate tracings to each of the maternal-fetal specialists; all supported her decisions. She brought the subject up to Kim again at lunch, even though they had already talked by telephone several times.

"Janet, you've got to stop. We've been over this too many times."

Kim was her best friend from medical school and was now head of maternal-fetal medicine at the university. She was forty-two years old, a chubby, smiling woman who wore loose fitting dresses to try to cover her weight. Unfortunately, the official physician's white coat ruined the effect. She was genuinely liked by her colleagues in St. Louis and around the country because of her bubbly, outgoing personality.

"Kim, I'm sorry." Janet didn't sound sincere. "This thing is really getting me down. I just don't know what to do. I can't get this baby out of my mind." She never said it aloud, not even to Mike, but she wondered if doing twenty-five deliveries in November and having that many scheduled in December affected her performance. She was even more tired than she had been earlier in the year, when Mike had first confronted her about cutting back.

"Janet, I'm sorry, too. You look exhausted. I'd bet there's more going on than this delivery. Tell me about Mike and the kids."

"There's not much to tell. The kids are growing, with the usual problems, and they're doing okay in school. Mike and I are working on that." She explained about the school problems. "I'm going to see their teachers this afternoon. The kids are a delight, though, when I have time to see them. Mike is fine, too, although he's pushing me pretty hard about slowing down and losing weight. We're pretty much okay otherwise."

"I can identify with the weight thing, Janet, and I'm sorry to hear about the kids and school. Now tell me about your practice. How's it really going?"

"Too well. I'm so darn busy, I don't have time to think. That's why I started canceling our lunches."

"That's too bad. Can't you cut back some?"

"I'm trying, but it's hard to turn away old patients when they have a new pregnancy or patients referred by other doctors. About the only hope I have is to limit my practice to just those people and not accept any other new patients. I've got to try something."

"Janet, haven't you been taking a day off once in a while, even if not every week?"

"No."

"How about an afternoon off?"

"No, there just hasn't been time, but I'm starting to now, as I told you."

"How many deliveries are you doing for crying out loud?" Kim persisted.

"Twenty-five to thirty a month. I try to keep it under twenty, but it's not working."

"How much GYN are you doing?"

"A couple of hysterectomies a week, plus some lap scopes and D&C's. I usually have two or three GYN patients in the hospital for a good share of the week."

"I don't see how you do it," Kim exclaimed. "The number of office visits you have to schedule for that many deliveries and that much surgery has to be overwhelming."

"I'm beginning to think so, too, and that's exactly why Mike's after me to change; I'm never home."

"I should think not. You'll never be able to keep this up."

"I've been thinking about moving my office into the building next to Memorial, where Mike is. That would save me the twenty to thirty minutes each time I have to go back and forth during the day. Using the overpass would be nice in bad weather."

"That's been one of the advantages at the med school—having the clinic and labor and delivery next to each other. We can cover both when we have to," Kim responded.

"I know, but I would really hate to leave where I am. I've been there so long, it's as much a part of me as my house is. I designed and decorated my suite the way I wanted it. Besides, none of the offices in the hospital building are as nice or as roomy. The rent is higher and parking for patients is much worse. The layout is already set, and redecorating is very expensive. So, I don't know."

"That's not your real problem, Janet, and you know it. You're trying to do too much. You've got to decide how to limit your practice so you can have more time for yourself. If you don't, you'll continue to have difficulties at home. Eventually, you'll have problems with your practice, too, because you're too tired or too rushed, or both. It's inevitable."

"That's sure a gloomy picture, but I know you're right. I'll try refusing new patients, I guess. Any other ideas you have are welcome," Janet said, sheepishly.

"Let's talk about something else and see if that won't help get this off of your mind. Tell me about your plans for Christmas," Kim suggested.

"We're not doing anything special. My parents are coming for ten days or so, as they usually do. Nothing else."

"That'll be nice. Your mother should help brighten your spirits."

"Why don't you join us for Christmas, Kim? We have plenty of room at our table, and you know my parents."

"If I can't go back home because of the call schedule, I'll definitely be there. I'll let you know in a couple of days. Since I don't have family here, I tend to get more days and nights on call during the holidays. As you might remember, school closes, but the deliveries keep right on going."

They talked about the holidays for awhile and went shopping for a short time. Janet stared vacantly into space; she rarely showed any enthusiasm for the pretty things on display.

"Janet, we can talk about this case as much as you want. Sorry I said anything. I'll help you in any way I can."

"Thanks, Kim. I knew I could count on you. Sorry to be so gloomy." She smiled halfheartedly. "Let's make lunch a regular thing, every Wednesday. I think I'm going to need it."

They parted on that note, but in spite of everyone's reassurances otherwise, Janet now felt the baby's problems had to be entirely her fault, that she had missed something or that she had not done all that she could or should have done. Her ego had definitely been bruised, and her usual cheerful personality took a nosedive. She wasn't eating well at all, and she looked tired and haggard.

Janet's visit to the teachers that afternoon was another shock. Carol's grades were slipping because she was also a disciplinary problem, talking in class and not paying attention. Michael was in the same boat on grades, but not as bad. Janet left for home somewhat depressed, realizing that she or Mike would have to be available on a daily basis before the kids developed habits that are difficult to change.

"Carol, I really don't understand how you could let yourself get into this kind of trouble. I can't believe it—talking so much, you disrupt the whole class. Who were you talking to?" Janet asked as soon as Carol got home.

"I'm sorry, Mom. I already told you that," she answered defensively.

"Who were you talking to? Please tell me."

"To that new girl who's as tall as me, so we're both in the back of the room. We weren't bothering anyone until Mrs. Krebs made a big stink."

"Carol, that can't be all. Your grades are down. You've always had As, and now you're getting Bs in almost everything."

"I've been helping the new girl, Marcie. She just can't keep up, and that's why we were talking, Mom."

"Honey, that's nice of you to help, but not when it hurts you and bothers others in the class. Besides, Mrs. Krebs is supposed to help Marcie, not you."

"I know that, but she's afraid to ask."

"Carol, I think you should take Marcie to talk to Mrs. Krebs. That will help her get started, and you can tell Mrs. Krebs that you're sorry about making noise, even if it was for a good reason. Then you can get back to your own studies. There's still time to get your grades back up this semester."

"Mom, I can't do that."

"Carol, yes you can. Otherwise, I'll have to go to school with you."

"No. I don't want you there. I'll take her, Mom. I'm sorry." She started crying. Janet hugged her close.

"Don't cry, honey. This will work out. What you tried to do was very nice. I'm proud of you for that. But let's let Mrs. Krebs take over. Okay?"

"I will, Mom." She stopped crying. "I'd better go study."

"Tell Michael to come in, will you?"

"Mike! Mom wants you," she yelled as she went through the door.

"Come in, Michael. Miss Johnson tells me you've been

using bad words in the hall. Is that true?"

"Yes. I'm sorry."

"What did you say?"

"Mom! Do I have to tell you?"

"Yes, I think you'd better."

"All I said was 'damn.' "

"Miss Johnson said she heard something else, too."

"I didn't say it. That was Tommy. All I said was 'damn.' "

"Michael, I'm sure it seems daring to use words like that. And I know you hear them on TV and at the movies once in awhile. That's why we're so careful about what you watch. But the truth is that nice people don't talk that way. If you think about it, you never hear Dad or me use those words or any other swear words. I'm sure you and Tommy think it's cute or grown up. But really, it's just dumb. Miss Johnson says you and Tommy have been talking in class, too. Is that true?"

"Yes, Mom. And he's also in trouble."

"I'm sure he is. Michael, I don't want to hear any more reports like this, and I want your grades to come back up. Okay?"

"I'm sorry, Mom." He didn't cry, but it clearly took a lot of effort. He consented to a hug and ran off.

Janet sat back in her chair, depleted. *Thank God these weren't major problems*, she thought. *I'll tell Mike as soon as he comes home, but I'm sure things well be okay for a while. We can take turns checking their homework.*

"Mike, I'm at my wits end trying to dissect this case." Later that day, Janet went through it all again with him. "I'm not sleeping very well, and you must notice I'm more 'out of sorts,' to use your phrase." They talked frequently about the Smith delivery at length after the children went to bed.

"Janet, I know. I've heard everything you've told me, and I can't find a flaw. You just didn't do anything wrong. You've got to let this go."

"Maybe that's true, but I sure didn't do something right," she countered.

"Oh, come on," he snapped. "You've presented the case at your departmental weekly conference at least twice, and even your worst critic couldn't find anything to pick on. The only criticism was what George Thomas wrote in the chart. I think you've got to accept that we occasionally have bad results that we can't ever explain and that are just not our fault. Two or three babies out of a thousand will get CP, and there's nothing anybody can do to prevent it, no matter how good they are. As a matter of fact, the incidence of CP is actually rising a little since so many premature babies are kept alive by our new technologies, at least that's what the latest reviews say."

"I don't care." Her face sagged. "I guess I'm one of those doctors who can't stand failure. My practice has really been very easy up until now, except for being too busy. I've never had a bad baby or any serious complications in either OB or GYN. Sure, I've delivered babies with problems like heart defects or spina bifida, but nothing as bad as this one. Besides, each of those times, we had some warning from the ultrasound exams. This baby was a total surprise, and that's so upsetting, so disturbing that I'm not certain I can tolerate the risk of it happening again."

"Janet, that's enough." He grabbed her by the shoulders. "The only way you can guarantee it not ever happening again is to stop practice entirely. I don't think that's what you want; at least, I hope not. Am I wrong?"

"Honey, I don't know." She avoided his stare. "Maybe I've lived in too protected an environment, first at the university and now at Memorial. I guess I haven't been in the real world. All I know is that I can't take this kind of upset. I put everything I had into this delivery, just like I do with all of them, and it was a bust, a total failure. Intellectually, I know the law of averages had to catch up, but I sure wasn't ready for it emotionally, not for this.

How do you handle failure, a death, or a bad result?"

"Janet, that's not fair. Death or bad results aren't necessarily failures. Preventable deaths or problems are. That's what all of us work so hard to avoid. I can't see that this result was preventable. I don't think you can, either."

"No. But we're trained to look at everything." She hung her head and gazed at the floor.

"So am I. Big deal. You've looked at everything and haven't found anything that could have caused CP. You couldn't prevent it, and reality finally caught up. Honey, you've got to stop this agonizing."

"What do you mean?" she flared.

"Doctors who worry too much can't make critical decisions when they're necessary. I don't think that's happening to you yet, but your constant worrying is beginning to bother me." Mike held his hand up as if to keep her away.

"Yeah, well, doctors who don't worry enough are even more dangerous. At least, I'll always get help," she mumbled.

"Come on. I never said that. Of course, you're right. I just don't want this to destroy you."

"It won't." She glared at him.

"Come here, Jan," he whispered as he reached for her.

She leaned into him and was buoyed by his strength and warmth.

"Thanks," she said, brushing his lips with a kiss and hugging him tightly.

"Janet, let's go upstairs and make love. Maybe that will make you feel better."

"I'm just too tired. Maybe another night," she answered, slowly pushing him away.

"Okay," he reluctantly answered. "Then why don't you go to bed now so you can catch up on some sleep? Maybe you'll feel better then."

33

"I'll try. Good night, Mike." She turned away.

Janet tossed and turned all night and felt worse in the morning. Breakfast was a chore; she snapped at Jenny and avoided the children. Rounds at the hospital were, at best, mercifully brief. She wondered why patients weren't smiling and talkative about their families. While she maintained her dress and appearance, it was obvious she was exhausted and distracted. At the office, some patients even began to question Nancy about Janet's behavior.

"Nancy, she doesn't smile at all. What's wrong?"

"Thanks for asking, Mrs. Sterling. I think she's fine, but she is tired—too many nighttime deliveries."

"Well, tell her to get some rest, for heaven's sake."

When Nancy told Janet, she was stunned.

"What do I do?" she cried. "I'm so tired, I can't see straight."

"Take some time off, doctor. I'm sure I can get someone to cover for you tonight or tomorrow night. At least you can try to get some rest then," Nancy suggested.

"Try for both, will you? That's a good idea."

While Nancy was calling, Janet thought about herself. *I'm so down right now that I just can't get enthusiastic about anything. Nothing's fun anymore, and I don't want to talk to anybody. I'm just dragging myself through the day.*

Nancy broke her reverie.

"Doctor, I've got you covered for tonight, for tomorrow night, and for the weekend. I hope that will give you a chance to catch up."

"Thanks, Nancy. That really should help. I know it'll make Mike happier, too."

Janet slept better that night after she and Mike made love, although it had been obvious that she lacked most of her usual enthusiasm. The following night she was back to fitful sleep, and she felt washed out in the morning.

Mike coerced Janet into going to the zoo with him and the children on Saturday afternoon. She declined a hamburger afterward, claiming she had a headache. They went to the Boston Pops, but she didn't pay much attention. On Sunday, she sat in the study and stared at a medical journal, waking with a start when it slid off her lap.

Janet dreaded her weekly call to her parents. She was pleased when all they talked about where their plans for Christmas. She knew she had to snap out of her funk by then, but she didn't know how. Carol and Michael were already excited, working on presents and cards for Granny and Poppy. But Janet's mental turmoil had her in a tizzy; she almost wished she could cancel their visit. *Thank God, Mike can help,* she thought. *He's good at it.*

The holidays and their visit went relatively smoothly. However, one afternoon when Janet was at a delivery, the rest of the family went for a walk. Granny soon skipped ahead with Carol and Michael, leaving Jim and Mike to talk.

"Mike, what's going on with Janet? She suddenly seems very distant the last two or three weeks, and she looks terrible. Margaret says she can't get anything out of her, and you know how close they are."

"Jim, I guess it's two things. She and I agreed last spring that she had to cut back on her OB practice, which she did, until the past three months. She's back up to twenty-five a month again. The second thing is a delivery she had earlier this month. The baby has CP, which was completely unexpected. Janet isn't handling it very well, and I'm not sure what to do to help her. We talk about it all the time, but it's usually just a rehash of previous conversations. She insists on blaming herself when everyone but one neonatologist says she's blameless."

"The practice part we suspected," Jim responded. "Needless

to say, we had no idea about the baby. From what I read, it's almost a given that she'll be sued."

"Jim, I'm sure that's true, but nothing's happened yet."

"I guess we shouldn't say anything until she tells us."

"Please don't. As it is, she'd be pretty unhappy to know I told you."

"I have to tell Margaret. Otherwise, we won't say anything. But now, at least, we know what's going on. Thanks, Mike."

"Come on, Poppy," Mike Jr. yelled. "You can walk faster than that."

"We're coming. Hold your horses." Jim galloped to him.

Janet had a fortunate lull in deliveries, allowing her to be with her family for Christmas dinner. Kim did join them, and everyone enjoyed the day.

Janet and Mike gave Carol a large dollhouse complete with lights. Her parents and Mike's parents added more than enough furniture, china, and kitchenware to keep Carol occupied. Michael was seemingly thrilled with the beginnings of a model train set which kept him, Mike, and Poppy busy. There were many other presents and more good food than they could ever eat.

Mike and Janet had cut their office hours between the holidays as much as possible, so they were able to be outside when there was a rare snow, go to movies, and explore a couple of museums.

After the holidays, her office opened full time, Janet found herself worrying again about her workload and about the Smith baby. To compensate, she tried to spend more time with the children. She didn't say much to Mike, but it was apparent that she was still upset. She even insisted on canceling a vacation they had planned to Hawaii because she was so disturbed.

5

Angie and Bill continued to have problems adjusting to each other and the baby. Christmas was particularly difficult. Angie visited the NICU twice a day, but with increasing dread and reluctance.

"Oh, Will, why don't you get better?" she whispered to him. "I keep hoping I'll walk in here and find all the tubes out, and you'll be waving your arms around. I want to hold you so much. What am I going to do with all the presents I bought you before you were born? Will you ever play with them?" Tears were streaming down her cheeks.

One of the nurses put her arm around Angie's shoulders, trying to console her.

"Thank you, but it doesn't help. He isn't going to get better, no matter what anyone does. Why did this have to happen? My whole pregnancy was so normal. Someone must have done something wrong."

The nurse left Angie staring at the crib and her apparition of a son, and went to tend to another baby.

Finally, Angie left, collected Wilma, who was watching soap operas in the waiting room, and led the way out of the hospital.

"Let's stop somewhere for a tree. You take care of it. I just don't think I could manage."

"I'd be happy to," Wilma answered cheerfully. "Is it okay if I get an artificial tree?"

"Sure. We'll put it in the family room. I have plenty of ornaments and lights at home, so don't get any of those."

"Angie." Bill was astonished when he came home. "Aren't we going to have a big tree in the front hall as usual? It won't seem like Christmas."

"Honey, it won't seem like Christmas no matter what we do." She shook her head glumly. "I just couldn't put my heart into it this year, so I asked Wilma to take over. I don't know what to do with all the things we got for the baby, but I know I don't want them in the front hall. I really don't want to see them at all."

"We haven't talked about it, but I assume we're not having a party this year either. I'm glad. I don't think it would help us much." He looked relieved.

"Bill, I couldn't even imagine having a party. Actually, I've refused all the other invitations we've received, too. I'm just not up to it, and I didn't think you were either."

"I'm not. This Christmas won't be very bright, I'm afraid. I went to the NICU today for a few minutes, and he hasn't changed at all. I almost couldn't go back to the office." Bill shook his head. "I'm sorry I said anything about the tree. This one will be just fine. Tell Wilma I said thanks."

"What are we going to do with the presents for Will?" Angie whispered.

Bill looked stricken and paused for a moment.

"Let's put them away until we can give them to him here at home. I got some too, you know."

"Okay, but under the tree will look pretty empty. I don't have much for you."

"That's okay, honey." He held her. "I haven't been able to get very interested in shopping either. Everything was going to be for Will."

"I know." She began to cry softly. Bill hugged her closely.

Angie let the maid and cook have time off, and she and Bill

went to the country club for Christmas dinner. She had wanted Wilma to go with them, but Bill refused. Once seated, she asked, "Why wouldn't you let me bring Wilma? It's not very nice to leave her there alone."

"I'm sure Wilma will find someone to be with. She seems to have quite a few friends, judging by the amount of time she spends on the phone. I wanted us to have a little time alone."

"I guess you're right. Thanks and Merry Christmas, Bill."

"Merry Christmas, sweetheart." He paused and then said, "Honey, let's let Wilma go temporarily or have her come for just a few hours in the daytime on weekdays. We can get her back when Will comes home. I need to have some time with you, without an outsider around. I know I can give you all the help you need. Okay?" Bill pleaded with her.

"Is that why you made her stay home, because you want to get rid of her?"

"No, I don't want to get rid of her. It's just that she's always around. She doesn't stay in the kitchen or another part of the house like the maid and the cook. She watches everything we do and say. When I come home, I want to be with you, not her."

"Sweetheart, I know that." Her body sagged as she reached for a tissue to dry her tears. "I'm sorry that I'm crying. I know Wilma's annoying to you, but she's all that keeps me going during the day. Don't you see, I'd go crazy if I have to sit there alone all day long, and I can't spend any more time at the hospital, like you. The cook and maid aren't the same. Give it some more time, please."

"I'll try . . ."

"You'd better," Angie snapped.

"I'll make sure I get home on time, but please wait and have dinner alone with me. Okay?"

"Sure. Now let's try to enjoy what we have left of Christmas."

"Yes, let's."

They did manage dinner together several nights that week and after, which helped. New Year's Eve was quiet also, unlike their usual celebration.

"Bill, I want to talk to this lawyer, Herbert Kline," Angie said, after the holidays were finally over. "I don't know what the right thing to do is, but I think we need advice from an expert to try to find out."

"Okay, okay," he answered.

"I've called a couple of friends whose husbands are lawyers, and they say that this firm is one of the best for malpractice. I want to know if that's what happened. Will you please arrange an appointment for whenever we can both go?"

"I'll call tomorrow." *Maybe this will help us get back on the right track,* he thought. "I'll also ask the company lawyer to look into this law firm, just to double-check them."

6

"I'm Herbert Kline. You're Mr. and Mrs. Smith?"

"Yes. Angie and Bill. Thank you for seeing us on such short notice."

Kline ushered them into his spacious office, which was furnished with an impressive collection of antiques and equally interesting paintings. As he seated them around a low table, Angie couldn't help but notice his large gold cufflinks, which perfectly complemented his three-piece navy-blue pinstripe suit. She focused on them throughout the meeting. Kline was tall and slender, with salt-and-pepper hair. He offered coffee or tea and asked how he could help. Both asked for black coffee, so Kline called the request in to his secretary.

Angie shifted uncomfortably in her chair and nodded to Bill to begin.

"Mr. Kline, our first baby was born almost six weeks ago, and he's not normal," Bill began, looking at Angie to be sure she was okay. "In fact, he has so many problems that he hasn't even come home from the NICU yet. He was born on his due date, December eighth, and everything had gone just fine during the pregnancy. However, in the labor room, the baby's heartbeat went way down, and the doctor just watched for over thirty minutes. She didn't do anything until it happened again. Then she finally did an emergency c-section." He kept pouring out information, almost without taking a breath and ignoring the secretary who brought in the coffee. "Our son was limp and didn't cry right, and he now almost certainly has cerebral palsy." Bill choked on the words. "We want to know what happened and what can be done about it. There has to be something the doctor did wrong for our baby to be so abnormal."

"Just a second, if you don't mind," Kline interrupted him. "Who's the doctor?"

"Dr. Jankowski, Janet Jankowski. She's the obstetrician."

Bill and Angie sat stiffly, looking very much ill at ease. After they both drained their cups, Kline offered them more from a carafe. He rested his pen on a legal pad, which was full of illegible notes, and began to carefully arrange the creases in his trousers. Bill didn't continue.

"I'll need to know a lot more to be able to advise you properly," Kline commented. "If I understand you correctly, Mr. Smith, you're saying that everything with the pregnancy was okay until this incident during labor and that the doctor delayed the baby's delivery. You feel the delay caused your baby to develop CP. Is that correct?"

"Yes. My pregnancy was absolutely uneventful all the way to term," Angie answered emphatically. "We went to see Dr. Jankowski three months before I became pregnant, and I followed all of her suggestions throughout my pregnancy. The delivery was planned, with an epidural, at Memorial Hospital. Everything was just fine with my labor until the baby's heart rate went down. She just didn't do anything. We begged her to do something, to take care of our baby." Angie was shrill, but absolutely dry-eyed.

"Take your time, Mrs. Smith," Kline said.

"When the neonatologist, Dr. George Thomas, came to my room early the next morning after Will was born, he told us about the delay Dr. Jankowski caused."

"Will, is that your son's name?" Kline interrupted.

"Yes, William N. Smith, Jr."

"Thanks. Go ahead."

"Dr. Thomas took over all of his care from then on. He was very direct when he said that it was her fault that Will had cerebral palsy." Angie paused to control her outburst. She took a couple of deep breaths and began again. "We got your name from Wilma James, the nurse who's helping me. We're here because we want to find out if there's anything that can be done. If there is, then we have to know all about it. This is hurting us terribly, and it has certainly ruined our son." Angie was almost strident.

"I'll need to know much more about you and your son before I can answer. Please tell me everything."

Bill and Angie spent the next hour talking about the pregnancy, their backgrounds, their jobs, their social life, and their hopes for the future. Kline interrupted occasionally to clarify a point, and they all had more coffee. Most of the time was spent talking about Angie's labor from the time her membranes ruptured until the cesarean section. Kline asked many questions and took several pages of notes. He was obviously well-informed about pregnancy, labor, and delivery.

"I'll look into this very carefully. Mrs. Smith, I'll need you to sign release forms directing all the doctors, especially Dr. Jankowski and the neonatology specialists, and the hospitals, to send copies of all their records of your prenatal care and delivery to me. This notifies them that an investigation is underway. That's fairly routine when a baby isn't normal. We are not announcing that we intend to file a suit. That remains to be seen. It only says that there's some question." Kline paused for coffee.

Angie and Bill stared at him.

"My partner, Jefferson Jones, will work with me on this. We work together closely on all our cases. Our regular fee is three hundred dollars an hour for each of us. I'm sorry he couldn't be here right now, but he's tied up on another case. As you might imagine, we will have to do a great deal of investigation, just to know if there really is merit to this case, although it certainly appears to me that there very well may have been negligence, based on what you've told me so far." Kline rearranged his notes.

"We are certain of it," Bill said.

"Since we will have to invest a large amount of time to get started, while my partner and I review those records and research the medical literature, I will charge you a retainer of ten thousand dollars, against which we will credit all of our hourly charges and expenses. There very well could be additional charges beyond the retainer. We must find experts to advise us, and we'll certainly talk to Dr. Thomas. If you two decide to pursue this case further and if a judgment or settlement is reached in your favor, our fee is thirty-five percent of anything recovered. I trust that meets with your approval." Kline looked at them expectantly.

"Mr. Kline, we'll have to talk about it. We expect to be billed for your time today. Please give us the release forms. If we decide to go ahead, I'll return the signed releases and a check for the ten thousand dollars, with instructions to proceed. Is that okay?" Bill finally asked.

Angie sat as if in a trance.

"That will be fine," Kline answered, almost breathing a sigh of relief. "Please understand that I can't be sure, but there appears to be a very strong likelihood that negligence did take place. If so, you deserve compensation. Do either of you have any questions?"

Angie and Bill looked at each other and slowly shook their heads.

"Then, I'll look forward to hearing from you. Thank you for coming by." Kline helped them with their coats and showed them out.

As they walked out, Bill took Angie's hand, but neither said anything until they reached the car. Once there, Angie opened like a flood gate.

"Bill, I'm really angry. After listening to the two of us tell the whole story for the first time, and not leaving anything out, I'm convinced that someone really screwed up. Dr. Thomas says it's Dr. Jankowski, and I think he's right. Our baby is never going to be okay; he may never even be able to come home to us. Dr. Jankowski delayed doing the c-section, and I think the maternal-fetal specialists are covering up for her. Dr. Thomas is the only one willing to tell the truth." She smeared her mascara by wiping her tears away.

Ever the practical one, Bill broke in.

"Slow down, sweetheart. My only problem is that we trusted Dr. Jankowski so much for so long that it seems a little unfair to change our minds this quickly. I'm concerned about the effect a lawsuit can have on us, too. It will cost a lot of money and proba-bly cause a lot of heartache, and I'm worried it could all be for nothing."

"Bill," Angie frowned at him, "are you backing out on me now? I don't understand you. Dr. Thomas told us that she waited too long. That should be enough. We're already left with nothing. The expense isn't worth talking about. Look what's happened to our lives, to me, and to us," Angie shouted at him.

They continued talking along these lines most of the way home.

"Okay. I agree," he finally said as they turned in the drive-way. "You sign the release papers, and I'll send them in with the check this afternoon."

"Really?"

"Yes, but now, what did you decide about your six-week checkup?"

"What do you care?"

"I'm sorry to pick, but I just want to make sure you're okay, honey. Don't you think it might be awkward going back to see Dr. Jankowski if we're planning to sue her?" Bill hugged her after he stopped the car.

"You're right, of course. Actually, I never did call for an

appointment. I just couldn't face her. I'll try to find someone else who'll see me and take over my care," she answered.

"Good. Angie, I didn't mean to sound like I don't want to pursue the lawsuit. I really do. I'm just afraid for you because I know how difficult the whole thing will be."

"Bill, I'll be okay. I promise," Angie said and got out of the car.

Angie did make a couple of calls after Bill left for the office, but she couldn't find an OB who was willing to see her after she explained that she had already delivered and that she wanted to switch doctors. She gave up trying after that.

Kline and Jones were an ill-matched pair at first glance. Kline, with impeccable manners and dress, had an aristocratic bearing. He was neat, precise, and very much in control. In contrast, Jones, a black man, was quite casual in his dress and demeanor, although he was highly disciplined about the practice of law. He was short, and his clothes were generally wrinkled and too tight because of his latest diet failure, so he habitually threw his jacket over a chair. His tie was always loosened, and his shirtsleeves rolled up. His office was cluttered with stacks of legal pads and briefs, and the furniture and decorations were comfortable, but functional, rather than stylish.

The lawyers' backgrounds were quite different also. Kline was the son of a tenant farmer and had gone to college on a hardship scholarship. Jones's parents were both professors at an elite Chicago university, so academic life was second nature to him. They met at law school in Chicago, where they both had academic scholarships, and became close friends, enough to want a practice together. They graduated near the top of their class. Neither wanted to stay in Chicago, having spent too many years there already, so they decided to set up their own practice in St. Louis, specializing in liability of all types. They were introduced to the city during an interview with one of the large firms they had turned down.

In spite of being reasonably busy, Kline and Jones made a point of working together on cases as much as possible, each using the other to his advantage. Usually, Kline played the tough-guy role, and Jones the good guy, but they could reverse parts, almost in the middle of a sentence. Over the years, they gradually limited their practice to medical and legal liability. Their ambition was to become successful enough to warrant hiring associate lawyers, plus they wanted to enjoy large incomes. They made time to meet at least a couple of times a week to discuss progress in all of their cases.

After the release forms and retainer were returned by the Smiths, Kline eagerly included his partner.

"Jefferson, I think I've really got a live one in this Smith case. This looks like the classic bad baby case that ought to go for a large settlement, one that will finally put us into the big time." Kline handed him his legal pad, his notes outlined precisely with bullet points. This time, they were neat and legible.

"Herb, I don't have anything new right now. All the old cases are on hold or moving slowly. That means I'll have plenty of time for this in the immediate future. Tell me more about this baby." Jones seemed equally enthusiastic.

"Well, Angie Smith," he explained, "apparently had a perfectly normal pregnancy, but then, during labor, there was a thirty-minute or so delay in response to a bad heart-monitor tracing, which resulted in a newborn with what looks like very severe CP." Kline reviewed all the allegations made by the Smiths. "After the delivery, George Thomas told them that it was Dr. Jankowski's fault. I hope he put it in the record, as we've suggested to him. Apparently there wasn't a problem with the anesthesia."

"I think you're right that this is a good case," Jones mused.

"I'm waiting on copies of the records now. I think we should probably ask Pete Wilson to look at them. He always seems to take the doctor's side of things, so we should get an idea of what the defense will attempt. I asked the Smiths for a ten-thousand-dollar retainer, so we'll be okay for awhile. Didn't we have something with this Dr. Jankowski a couple of years ago?"

"Yeah, we did," Jones answered after reflecting for a moment. "She referred a clinic patient under her care at Memorial to University Hospital so the delivery would take place close to the NICU. I've forgotten what the complication was, but I can look it up if we need to know. University Hospital threatened to sue the patient for nonpayment of the bill, since her insurance wasn't enough to cover it. Louise Washington, the patient, came to us to sue Dr. Jankowski to get funds to pay the hospital. She wanted to claim an unnecessary cesarean section because both she and her baby did so well. Actually, Dr. Jankowski's care was textbook perfect." Jones explained the case to Kline. "We negotiated a settlement with University Hospital instead. The Washingtons paid seventy-five hundred dollars of their remaining bill, which was well over twenty thousand dollars. Everyone came out ahead."

"That's interesting, but I doubt it will be any help since nothing was filed and no settlement was made by Dr. Jankowski. I'll keep you posted on this new one when all the records are in."

In the weeks following their decision to enter the legal arena, Angie and Bill coasted along in their private lives. Angie grew stronger, and Bill worked harder, but they weren't any closer.

"How was your day, honey?" Bill asked each evening.

"The same. We went to the hospital twice, as usual. There's no change. Since the weather was nice, Wilma and I went for a walk. I'm feeling better physically." Her cheeks were pink, and she looked good, having just come in.

"Your boss asked me today when you're coming back. I told him I didn't think it would be right away and that I'd talk to . . . "

"I don't know how I can even consider that right now." Angie grimaced. "It's been barely seven weeks since the c-section. I'll think about it. Tell him it won't be before eight weeks, and more likely ten or twelve."

"I'm sure that will be okay."

"I'm not offering a choice," she interrupted.

"He really wants you completely recovered before you return. The training group is holding together well for now," Bill continued.

Their weekends were somewhat better, because Bill stayed at home and tried to get Angie out of the house to do something, anything, in addition to visiting the hospital.

"Honey," Angie suggested on Saturday, "let's go to a movie and then go to the NICU. If we go see the baby first, I won't want to do anything after that."

"Okay. The movie starts at two o'clock, so let's go now. We can get lunch at the mall and look in the bookstore beforehand."

"I'd like that. I'll be ready in ten minutes." Angie smiled at him.

They enjoyed lunch, shopping, and the movie, but the NICU was a total letdown.

"Oh, Bill, he looks terrible. He's hardly gained any weight. What are we going to do?"

"I don't know. I'm completely baffled. Kline hasn't called, so we don't know what he's doing. Dr. Thomas doesn't talk to us much and isn't very encouraging when he does. I don't know what to expect." He shook his head.

"Honey, let's go home. I can't stay here another minute."

Bill started visiting the NICU a couple of times each week on his own and always joined Angie on the weekend. Each time, they went through the same tiresome litany, asking if there had been any progress made.

Then, one evening when Bill came home, he found Angie visibly upset. Her face was red, and it looked as if she had been crying for quite awhile.

"Honey, what happened?" Bill rushed over to her.

Angie smiled halfheartedly and smeared her face, wiping away her tears.

"I finally talked to Dr. Thomas. He said that Will isn't making any progress at all and that he hasn't made any of the landmarks in development that he should have made. Then he said that Will almost certainly will be severely retarded. He really didn't offer any hope at all. I'm overwhelmed, even though I think we both knew this was coming."

"Angie, I'm so sorry. That makes me even more certain about the lawsuit." Bill pulled her close and kissed her.

Later, when both had a cocktail in hand, Bill approached her.

"Sweetheart, let's make love. It's been so long."

"After dinner, dear. Wilma wants to go somewhere, so your timing is perfect." She clung to him, returning his kiss with equal enthusiasm. Then she went into the kitchen to survey the cook's dinner plans, found everything to her satisfaction and told the cook and the maid that they could leave early.

Angie and Bill lingered over the last of a bottle of wine, dessert, and then coffee.

"Sweetheart, this was really nice," Bill whispered, staring into her eyes. "We haven't had a pleasant evening like this in months."

"I know, honey," she answered, returning his gaze. "I enjoyed it, too. Let's go sit by the fire."

Bill put on several of their favorite CDs, and they sat in front of the fire, kissing and caressing. However, their lovemaking wasn't successful. Angie couldn't respond, and she finally pushed him away.

"Bill, I'm sorry. I don't have any interest anymore. All I think about is that damned doctor and what she did to Will. I'm really sorry, because this was a wonderful evening, but let's wait awhile longer."

7

Kline went to Thomas's office, which was stacked, as usual, with copies of medical records, depositions, medical journals, and other papers.

Thomas cleared a chair for him and started discussing the details of the Smith case with him.

"Are you absolutely certain that this baby was damaged during labor and not before?" Kline asked after a few minutes. "We think the entire case hinges on that issue." He held up his hand to keep Thomas from interrupting, a frequent occurrence. "Some of my recent research indicated that medical opinion may be changing to the point of view that the damage causing CP, whatever it is, probably occurs before labor. If that's the case, we need to focus our attention on the prenatal period, which will make this case much more difficult."

"Yes, I am quite certain, Mr. Kline, beyond a shadow of a doubt. As you well know, I'm certified in neonatology and have made a specialty of these types of cases. I have many years experience and am thoroughly conversant with the pertinent medical literature. For those reasons, I am one hundred percent sure of my statement in relation to when the CP was caused in this baby."

Thomas raised his hand to keep Kline from commenting. "However, since I'm not certified in maternal-fetal medicine, you'll have to get someone who is an expert in that field to testify for you. This will add strength to the case. Dr. Joseph Segal at Cloud View Hospital has given despositions and testified with me many times before and certainly will again. As I recall, all those cases were with other legal firms. At any rate, he is an expert in maternal-fetal medicine, with all the proper credentials, and I recommend him highly. That should be sufficient to win this case."

"That's very interesting. I was already considering asking him. Thanks for the reference," Kline commented.

"Now, then, this baby certainly was normal before labor began. All the testing done throughout her pregnancy was quite satisfactory. We have absolutely nothing to indicate otherwise. She was not a smoker. Unfortunately, there wasn't a nonstress test done, but I'm sure it would have been normal. Believe me, I've thoroughly reviewed the prenatal records. I think Dr. Jankowski simply did not pay close enough attention during labor, even though she was apparently in labor and delivery the whole time."

"She was. I already checked that," Kline answered.

"My guess is she was chatting with the residents or nurses, rather than looking at the monitor. When she finally did notice something out of the ordinary, she didn't react quickly enough. In fact, she didn't take any significant steps for thirty minutes."

They went through the case again in more detail, page by page.

"I might agree with you about looking at the prenatal care as the cause if this case weren't so blatantly mishandled. Dr. Jankowski was clearly derelict in her job performance." Thomas was emphatic. "Remember, the medical literature does not say that all CP begins before the onset of labor. I don't think you'll have a bit of trouble getting Dr. Segal, or someone equally knowledgeable, to verify that in court, if it goes that far."

"You'd better leave the legal business to us, although I'm pleased you're so confident," Kline interjected, a little overpowered by Thomas. "If this proves to be as much of a sure thing as you think, we hope to arrange a settlement without having to go through all the expense, bother, and delay of a trial. The Smiths want a rapid conclusion also. I assume you'll be willing to give a deposition and to testify for us, if it should be necessary?" he asked.

"Yes, of course I will. However, I must inform you that I've raised my fees, since I do so much legal work." Thomas handed him a schedule. "Also, you do know that I inform the parents every time I think there's a problem with the care provided by an obstetrician, and I always endeavor to write it in both of the charts. Unfortunately, the need to do so occurs more often than it should. Medical practice certainly deteriorates each year."

"We're aware of your opinions, and we're aware that the obstetricians in St. Louis and in the surrounding two states have no love for you," Kline observed quietly. "One other thing. I hear that my colleagues among plaintiff attorneys are losing more CP cases recently. If you're involved with any of those, we'll stop using you."

"So far, I haven't lost any cases for you and Jones. It's been a pretty nice arrangement for all of us. As stated on the schedule, my fees are now five hundred dollars an hour to review records, five thousand dollars for each deposition, and ten thousand dollars per half-day to testify at a trial, plus expenses. I need plenty of notice so I can arrange my schedule, but I promise to be available. I trust this is satisfactory?" Thomas asked expectantly.

"I'm certain it will be. I'll be in touch." Kline gathered his things and left.

Kline knew that he could subpoena Thomas as a witness to fact, as the primary physician for the baby, and that he didn't have to pay a witness to fact. He knew that he could probably get away without an outside expert, since Thomas had obligingly written his opinion in both the records. However, this case would certainly be much stronger with a designated expert medical witness for neonatology, and he felt that combining both witness types in one, Thomas, was the best strategy, even though he was expensive. He knew that the potential recoverable damage award more than justified this decision.

After bidding Kline good-bye, Thomas settled back in his chair. He felt quite confident that he'd convinced Kline of his worth. He had realized early on that his New Zealand accent was of benefit when testifying, in spite of his trying to hide it otherwise. He made a lot of money, working exclusively for plaintiffs.

For several years, he had been telling parents of his concerns and then testifying for them in any subsequent legal action. As might be expected, he saw no conflict of interest in this, either with his obstetrical colleagues or with his primary mission of being a teaching neonatologist at the university. Well more than a third of his time was spent in legal work, and the income he earned testifying was more than double his university salary. He realized he was known in the medical profession as a "whore" or "hired gun," someone who would testify for the plaintiff in any case, with or without merit, strictly for money, and this didn't concern him in the least.

After all, he was an expert at convincing the judge and jury of his veracity and knowledge about abnormal babies, and the possibility that he might be wrong didn't bother him. He felt that these babies and parents deserved compensation, and he was more than pleased with the income he derived from their lawyers.

8

Janet was even more devastated by the looming realization that the Smith baby would most likely result in her first professional liability lawsuit. She had visited the university NICU late at night several times. After midnight, she was certain she had little risk of having to talk with the Smiths or anyone else. Her fears concerning the extent of the abnormalities in the baby were more obvious each time. Janet's overwhelming, but illusory, hope was that the Smiths wouldn't consider a lawsuit, that the whole thing was just a bad dream.

She sat at her consultation-room desk, signing charts, checking dictation, and reading her mail, as was her habit around noon each day if there was a lull in her patient schedule. She slowly ate an apple, hoping to lose some of the weight she had gained over the past six months. The request from Kline and Jones, marked personal and confidential, was with that morning's mail. Screwing up her courage, she opened it and found her worst fears confirmed. It contained the formal request for a copy of her records, and it also indicated that similar requests had been sent to the other doctors and hospitals involved.

Her hands shaking, Janet tried to call Mike but found him swamped, so she didn't leave a message for him to call her back. She decided to tell him that evening instead. She then called Clark Newton, the attorney who was head of the Risk Management Committee at Memorial Hospital and at whose instruction she had Darlene make a copy of her office records for him. Newton responded that he would send all the required documents to

Kline and Jones. Memorial and the doctors who worked there were jointly self-insured, meaning that each doctor and the hospital contributed to a pool set aside for defense and any payout necessary. Legal support was provided by the hospital. He asked her to come by late that afternoon.

"Dr. Jankowski, I'm sorry to get to know you this way. Please call me Clark. May I call you Janet?" He showed her in just after five o'clock.

She nodded and sank down slowly into the chair he offered her. "Janet, these cases are never fun, and they are not all that easy to predict. I wish you had told us about this right after it happened, although I doubt we could have done very much. But sometimes we can help the parents adjust, connect them with a support group, that sort of thing. It might have helped."

Janet seemed to melt into the chair. Her lower lip quivered. She shook herself and took a couple of deep breaths. She explained the case briefly.

"Did anyone else report this to you?" she asked tentatively, annoyed with herself for forgetting.

"No, they didn't. I'll have a talk with the head of the pediatrics department. If what you tell me about the Smith case proves to be true, that the maternal-fetal group supported all your decisions and continue to do so now, we have a good chance," he encouraged her. "However, I have to tell you that Kline and Jones have a reputation for being very tough; they don't pursue a lawsuit unless they feel that there's considerable merit in their case or at least a reasonable probability of winning a settlement. They'll be looking for experts to back their allegations. And, unfortunately for us, they're pretty successful at winning liability suits. We'll find out more as we get into this further, especially during discovery. What questions can I answer for you?"

"This is my first real exposure to any kind of legal action.

What should I do now, and what can I expect?" Janet was jittery and very upset. Outwardly, she appeared to be in reasonable control, but internally, she felt far from it. Her stomach was doing flip-flops.

"What do you mean by first 'real exposure'?" Newton queried.

Janet told him about the patient two years earlier who had been sent to the university.

"I'm glad that worked out," Newton answered, "even though there was little chance you would've lost such a suit anyway. I remember my associate telling me about it at the time. Do you remember the law firm involved?"

"No, I don't. I'm sorry. I can look it up back at the office."

"That's okay. I can find out, although I doubt it makes any difference."

"That's the only legal inquiry of any kind I've ever had."

"I'm glad. I can tell you about a number of things to expect in this case, but I'm sure I'll miss some, and others will be changed at the last minute."

"Go on."

Newton seemingly counted his points on his fingers.

"The first will be a meeting with the Risk Management Committee, probably next Friday, a week from tomorrow. I'll let you know in the morning. We usually begin at one-thirty every Friday, and you should plan on the whole afternoon. The big problem there is that it will take time out of your office schedule, and because you will meet with the committee so soon, you will have to reschedule a number of patients."

"I'll do whatever I have to do."

"Second, it's a meeting with your peers in other disciplines. They will question you intensively, and that may be upsetting and possibly embarrassing for you. They won't be nasty to you, but they will ask tough questions. Their major decision is whether to recommend fighting it or settling."

"You mean they could recommend giving in? I didn't do anything wrong. I don't know if I can stand that." Her face grew drawn and paled as her despair deepened.

"Unfortunately, you don't really have a choice," Newton continued, unruffled. "Since we're self-insured, each of us must abide by the decisions of the committee, which reports to the Memorial Hospital Board of Trustees. Our committee is just like the claims committee of an insurance company, which administers the funds available for defense or payout. That's what you purchase when you contribute to the pool each year. The advantage is that we are more in control of our own cases, and it is less expensive, since we do all the administrative work internally."

Janet leaned forward to hold her head in her hands, elbows resting on the table.

"This is worse than I imagined."

"The committee and the hospital board are usually inclined to fight claims, unless there's clear-cut negligence. However, the price of fighting cases has been skyrocketing, so they have occasionally recommended settlement. Frankly, I rather doubt they'll be for settling with the Smiths, but we have to wait to find out. We don't have to report this to the National Practitioner Data Bank yet. That comes only if we do settle or lose in court."

"I've read about that. If I lose in any way, it becomes a permanent public record, isn't that right?" Janet groused.

"I'm afraid so."

"You can count on my raising all kinds of commotion at any suggestion of settlement. I didn't do anything negligent, and I won't give up," she declared.

"I hear you, and I'll tell the committee. Actually, the stigma of being recorded in the National Practitioner Data Bank makes any kind of settlement, just to save money, very unlikely. None of our physicians would agree to that." Newton smiled at her.

"What happens next?"

"Next, Kline and Jones and I will each find experts to help us. If their experts agree with them that there is cause for action, they will formally file a lawsuit. They will probably use Thomas as an expert witness, since he already agrees with them." Newton grimaced. "Once that's done, each side gets the chance to take depositions. As I'm sure you know, depositions are sworn testimony, just like in court in front of a court reporter. However, they're usually not as harsh, because there isn't a judge or jury to impress, just the lawyers and the person being deposed."

"I'm listening," Janet said quietly, lifting her head briefly.

"Each side tries to find out what's going on with the opposition. They will depose you, and I'll depose the Smiths, and each side will depose the other's experts. This, again, will take time from your office work, at least half a day for your deposition. You'll have to prepare by studying all the records, repeatedly. Then you'll have to read and reread all the testimony from all the other depositions, and take time with me and with the committee to discuss all of them. I'll find medical articles for you to read, and I hope you will do some additional research on your own."

"I'll look at everything I can get my hands on," Janet said.

"Finally"—he was running out of fingers—"if it goes that far, we go to trial, and that will take several days or even a couple of weeks out of your life, both for court and for preparation. I haven't said anything about the mental turmoil this will cause, but I think you already have some idea about that."

"How long does this process usually take?" Janet asked glumly.

"It can take months to years. The average is two to three years. The big reasons for delay are either crowded court dockets or the weaker side prolonging things in the hope of forcing a settlement more to their advantage. Actually, each side tries to build as strong a case as possible, which requires a lot of time for research. All the attorneys are busy with other cases, which may also cause a conflict or a delay. Finally, the expert witnesses have busy schedules, and they will need time to get ready. They can be a problem."

"Having this drag out for months or even a year sounds horrible," Janet whispered.

"I think this case will proceed much faster, however, because Kline and Jones think they have a sure thing and will therefore push hard for an early settlement. We don't want any delays, because delay only increases expense, no matter what the outcome is." Newton paused.

Janet continued to stare at him intently.

"We'll just have to see. I'll do my best to keep you informed, and I'll try to give you plenty of notice to reschedule your office visits." He paused again. "One other thing. Any communication of any kind about this case must go through me. Please don't do or say anything without my permission. That way, I'll know what's going on, so I can keep us out of trouble."

"Clark, I hope you understand how upset I am by this," Janet said.

"I understand. Keep in touch, Janet. I'm here to help you."

"Thanks very much. I'll come by at least once a week just to talk things over. Good-bye." Janet walked out slowly and went directly home.

Once in the comfort of her study, Janet cried softly. She asked the nanny to take care of dinner, and she tried to explain to the children what was going on. Her stomach was churning, and she had heartburn as bad as when she was pregnant.

Mike found her still there when he came in.

"This has to be one of the worst days I've ever had," she cried to him.

He tried to calm her as she told him about the letter and her meeting.

"Clark Newton, our attorney, tells me they could decide it's cheaper to try for a settlement with the Smiths. I couldn't believe it when he said that." She related her conversation with Newton.

"When do you get to meet with the committee?" Mike stood behind her chair, massaging her neck and shoulders.

"Next Friday, most likely. He's supposed to let me know in the morning. I'll have to cancel my office patients on top of everything else. Clark warned me how much time the process would take. That feels good, Mike."

"I know about the time factor. Do you remember a few years ago when my senior partner was sued? I had to cover for him. I guess it cost him at least six weeks in lost time and income. Plus, it really tore him up emotionally, even though he won."

"Thanks. That's just what I didn't need to hear. But I guess it's better to know all this up front." Janet's eyes were dry, but she still sat hunched over in her chair.

"Unfortunately, honey, I think you'll be surprised anyway. Each of these cases is different."

Slowly, she relaxed, as he continued massaging her shoulders and neck.

"Mike, I'm sure you're right. I just hoped I wouldn't find out about all of this in such an impersonal way. If you don't mind, let's go out to a quick dinner and a movie. I need to do something that doesn't require any brain function, and I don't think I can talk about this anymore without crying. Okay?"

"Sure. You know I'll do anything I can to help. Tell me as much as you want as the case proceeds. Let's talk to the kids a little and then go."

They went to Garibaldi's, and Janet suffered through Vince's attempts at welcoming them. She pushed the food around her plate, virtually unresponsive to Mike's conversation. Finally, he simply stopped talking.

Janet fell asleep in the movie and was then awake most of the night. She thought about the Smith delivery over and over, then the threatened lawsuit, and, finally, the possibility of losing.

Each thought upset her more, so she got out of bed and crept down to the kitchen for a glass of milk, hoping that would help her stomach. When she was in medical school, Janet had tried outlining her thoughts as a way for preparing for exams. Even that didn't help, since she was convinced that nothing reasonable could have been done differently that would have had any bearing on the outcome of the delivery.

So she stayed awake. Finally, she went to the family room to lie down on the couch to avoid disturbing Mike.

Mike awakened Janet at six-thirty when he came downstairs.

"Janet, how long have you been there? Did you sleep at all?"

"Since three, and I last saw the clock at five, so I guess I slept an hour or so. I feel lousy. Maybe a shower will help."

"I'm out, so go ahead. I'll get breakfast for us."

"Thanks, Mike."

They were on their way at seven-thirty, after saying good morning to the nanny and the children. Each had to see patients at Memorial before going to the office.

Janet was nowhere close to any kind of organized thinking about her schedule. So far, she hadn't even been able to contain her emotions enough to be reasonably efficient at the office. Unfortunately, her inefficiency made her later each evening.

She wanted to call her parents, but felt she couldn't. She was certain her father had never been sued, and the embarrassment at having to tell him was too formidable for her to take on.

Lunch with Kim on Wednesday was somber.

"Janet, you won't fall apart," Kim exclaimed. "Quit hugging your elbows. You're making me feel bad, too." She reached out for Janet's hand.

"Kim, I'm having a lot of difficulty coming to grips with this whole thing. I find myself sitting like this at the office, staring at the wall. Nancy has to nudge me to get me going."

"That won't help. Come on, let's take a walk. Maybe that will get you to liven up a bit." Kim stood up and pulled Janet's hand.

"Kim, I can't." Janet pulled her hand away. "I've got to go back to the office to review records to get ready to go to the risk-management meeting. Sorry."

"I understand. Call me any time."

"I will. And I'll see you at lunch next week." Janet trudged to her car.

9

Peter Wilson, M.D., was a black man who had trained in obstetrics and gynecology at the university fifteen years earlier, and who had set up his office in a black middle-class area near Community Hospital, where he practiced. He had been reasonably successful financially, enough to satisfy him and his family, and he was often overwhelmed with patients because he did not turn anyone away, regardless of their financial status. Wilson and Jones had met soon after they began their respective practices and had become close friends.

"Pete, how are you?" Jones asked when he entered Wilson's office.

"I'm too busy, Jefferson, but doing fine."

"Did you look at the records I sent you?" Jones asked after they sat down.

"Yes, I did. The Smiths may be a bit of a problem for you."

Jones frowned at hearing this.

"When I look at the fetal heart monitor tracings," Wilson continued, "it's pretty obvious that the baby had lost beat-to-beat variability from the point where Dr. Jankowski began monitoring her, just after Mrs. Smith came to the hospital. That's the only thing out of order I can really find, but I think it's important. It means that there's a pretty good chance that this baby was already compromised before Mrs. Smith started labor." Wilson paused.

"You mean there wasn't any delay like Thomas and the Smiths claim?" Jones seemed incredulous.

"I really don't think so, but I'm not a maternal-fetal specialist. However, from what I know of the standard of care, Dr. Jankowski was well within normal limits. There was one bad dip, but the heart rate came right back up to normal and stayed there for the next thirty minutes. When the second dip came, she went as fast as anyone could, and she got the baby delivered in under twenty minutes from the time she said go. That's pretty good. Most OBs and hospitals can't do that."

"Pete, this isn't what I want to hear," Jones said.

"So, I don't know if you've got a case or not. If it's certain this baby was okay on admission—remember the lack of beat-to-beat variability—then there's some room to claim that going to a c-section earlier could have made a difference. From what I've read recently in medical journals, this may be difficult to prove. I'd get a maternal-fetal person to look at these records."

"Pete, you're telling me the defense may be able to use our points for their side, aren't you?"

"I guess I am," he answered slowly. "Jefferson, you can expect the defense to pick up on the beat-to-beat variability as one of their major points. The other point will be that one dip, with recovery, is okay, as long as vigilance is increased, which certainly happened here."

"Well, George Thomas ignores the variability and thinks that the first change in heart rate is important, and that there was subsequent delay, which was directly the cause of the CP," Jones answered. "He is very emphatic. He also suggested Joseph Segal as the maternal-fetal expert. What do you think?"

"They're both whores," Wilson exclaimed. "Pardon my language, Jefferson. I guess it depends on how much you want to win this case. They will both agree, for money, with almost anything. As I've said, this case bothers me, but I just can't put my finger on it. You might want to find another maternal-fetal expert to see if there's agreement on the delay. Let me know what you decide."

"I will, Pete, and thanks. Send us a bill, please," Jones said.

"I wouldn't be surprised if the so-called experts charge a lot more than I do. That's why they're willing to testify. Jefferson, I don't know how you keep doing this stuff. The entire medical profession hates you two, except for Thomas and people like him."

"How about I ask the girls to work out something for this weekend?" Jones asked, clearly avoiding the issue.

"That sounds great."

"Good. I hope to see you then."

Clark Newton was a fifty-eight-year-old, bearded, pipe-smoking, gruff man, who wore baggy brown suits with tobacco burns on them. He was tall, a little heavy, and well-tanned and wrinkled from a lot of time outdoors. He said hello to the rest of the risk-management group and asked the staff person to summarize the case in some detail for the physicians who had not yet seen copies of the records.

"The Smith baby was born here and now has CP or something very similar to it. Dr. Janet Jankowski was the OB. The baby was in difficulty right from birth." The staff member gave all the details in thirty minutes. "I asked one of the maternal-fetal people from the university to look at the monitor tracing, and she said that the only thing she could see was some lack of beat-to-beat variability from the time Mrs. Smith came in. But she said that there was nothing to fault with Dr. Jankowski's management, and she emphasized that there was no delay. She feels there is no reason for this threat of a lawsuit."

"For the record, who's the attorney for the Smiths?"

"Kline and Jones. Kline signed the request."

"Kline is usually thorough. It's too bad he does this sort of thing for a living, even if he does lose almost half of his cases. Still, it sure raises hell in doctors' lives. I'd bet they talked with Pete Wilson on this one, since he and Jones are close friends. He should say the same thing as our maternal-fetal person. Do we have any idea who their experts are?" Newton asked.

"George Thomas saw the baby the morning after the delivery, and he is still directing his care at University NICU." So far, the staff person was doing all the talking. "He will almost certainly be their neonatology expert. He seems to pretty regularly take care of abnormal babies and then testify as an expert for their parents. By the way, the baby is still in the university NICU, because he won't suck and has to be fed through a nasogastric tube. Thomas is talking about putting in a gastrostomy tube, so that he can be discharged."

"What's this about a gastrostomy tube? I thought that was used for terminal cancer patients?" Newton asked. *I don't like the sound of this one bit. No matter where the fault lies, a baby who has to have a hole in his stomach to be fed looks so bad in court that we might lose, even if we're completely correct in our management*, he thought.

"The idea is the same," one of the physician members answered. "A permanent connection between the stomach and belly wall is made with a hole for a feeding tube. It avoids the risk of the baby gagging or choking on a tube through its nose and throat."

"What's with Thomas? He seems to be doing a lot of testifying against doctors, including our own. I can think of one or two cases against us just in the last couple of years. Isn't there any way to stop him?" Newton thought out loud, even though he knew the answer. "Faculty regard the right to testify for either side in lawsuits as a part of academic freedom and freedom of speech, no matter how much trouble it causes for us or for our referring doctors," Newton continued, answering himself.

"On top of that, the chair of pediatrics is unwilling or hasn't been able to talk to him. Thomas is on a crusade to compensate the parents of every bad baby, which may be commendable, but he is also earning much more in the legal arena than the university pays him. Perhaps he confuses zeal with greed. Do we have any idea who their maternal-fetal expert will be?"

"Almost certainly Joseph Segal at Cloud View. He and Thomas seem to come together as a package," the staff person answered.

"There's a slimy one. What's the name of our maternal-fetal woman you had look at the records? Is she tough enough to help us?" Newton asked.

"Kimberly Workman," staff quickly answered. "She's very good, and she and Thomas have tangled before. CP has been her major research interest for many years. She's one of the leading authorities in the country."

"That's encouraging, for a change." Newton smiled for the first time. "Let's get her officially involved. I've worked with her before, and I know she'll do well. I assume she didn't have anything to do with Mrs. Smith's care?"

"No, she didn't." Staff hesitated. "The only possible problem is that she and Janet Jankowski are close friends. I'll get her full copies of the records today."

"Their friendship shouldn't make any difference," Newton declared. "Defendants tend to welcome friends as their experts because they trust them. Besides, the OB-GYN community is too small to avoid it."

Newton asked the committee to be prepared to meet weekly until more information was in. He expressed his reservations about the case.

"A bad baby case is always difficult because most people expect pregnancies to end perfectly. This one will be even more sticky because of the feeding tube. Let's really work on this one. Dr. Jankowski will meet with us next Friday. I talked with her yesterday. She is certain her care was correct."

The University Hospital attorney was Chester House, who,

at thirty-two, was relatively young for such a major position. He was quietly anxious to prove his merit, having been in the position for just over four months.

House and the University Hospital Risk Management Committee met to discuss the Smith case. This committee, like the one at Memorial, was made up of five physicians representing the major departments, two administrators, and the legal staff.

"Tell me about this new case. I understand it's from OB," House said.

"That's right. Mrs. Smith delivered a boy at Memorial who has CP. We were involved as consultants, both during her pregnancy for genetic counseling and during labor when there was question about the fetal heart-rate tracing. The primary obstetrician was Janet Jankowski at Memorial," staff explained at length. "We continue to be involved because the baby has been here in the NICU for almost three months, and he still can't suck or swallow. They're thinking about putting in a feeding gastrostomy tube so that he can be sent home. George Thomas is the primary neonatologist, and he also appears to be an expert for the plaintiff."

"He's one of ours, isn't he?"

"That's right. But he does a lot of plaintiff work."

"Who's the plaintiff attorney for this case?"

"Kline and Jones. Kline seems to be heading this one."

"He's good from what I hear. Will we have trouble with Memorial?" House asked.

"We haven't in the past, and we are pretty close with them," staff answered. "A lot of the physicians from both hospitals go back and forth to see patients. Maybe you should talk with their attorney, Clark Newton. They'll need our backing on this."

"I'll do that. Is there anything else related to this case?"

"Yes. Dr. Jankowski was involved with another case a couple of years ago that came to nothing." The staff person explained the details.

"Do you remember the attorney involved?"

"The same firm, but that time, it was Jones."

"I really don't like the idea of suing an innocent party to gain leverage over another. These guys won't stop at anything. Maybe it was all a bluff, but you shouldn't do that sort of thing unless you're willing to go all the way. It's a matter of principle," House emphasized. "That makes me even more interested in helping Memorial win this case. I'll talk with Newton and look at the records as soon as I can. Who should we use here as our maternal-fetal expert?"

"I think Kimberly Workman has already seen the Smith records for Newton. She didn't take care of Mrs. Smith, so she can help both of us."

"Good. I'll talk to her, too."

House called Kim after the meeting and found that she was already familiar enough with the details to tell him that the case would be difficult, especially because of Thomas, but that she believed Janet had been correct in all of her management. House arranged to meet with Kim after she had gone through the records again in more detail. He commented again about Thomas being a plaintiff witness against his own colleagues. She agreed with him about Thomas, but neither seemed to know what to do about him.

House called Newton next.

They talked at length and arranged to meet soon, when both had completed a review of the records.

"I'll help you in any way I can," House said. "I'm surprised we don't seem to be included in this, since our maternal-fetal people were consultants over at Memorial. Maybe they're afraid of taking on both of us." The request for records was not sent directly to the university's maternal-fetal medicine specialists, only to Memorial Hospital.

"It's more likely they feel they have an open-and-shut case

against Dr. Jankowski. I don't think so. I'm certain Thomas and Segal will have them so pumped up that they're ignoring you guys; at least I hope so. That's a mistake. Let's hope there are more mistakes," Newton answered.

"If you don't mind, I'd like to be there when you depose Jankowski, Workman, and Thomas, especially Thomas, if it goes that far," House requested. "I'm really upset that he's testifying so frequently against his colleagues here. If I can catch him making a mistake, maybe I can stop him in the future."

"You're more than welcome to come." Newton was pleased. "In fact, you're welcome to question any of them. I'll make the introductions at the appropriate time."

"Sounds good. See you soon."

10

Janet became more melancholy as it became increasingly obvious to her, and to everyone else, that a lawsuit would certainly be filed. She walked, sat, and talked slumped over and with a vacant look on her face. She rarely noticed others in the hospital halls, and she often didn't respond to greetings. When confronted by Kim or Mike, she whined, "I don't feel good. I haven't got any energy. I can barely move, let alone hold my head up." These episodes increased in number and length.

Janet was terribly upset about the meeting with the Memorial Hospital Risk Management Committee. She appeared to be in tight control, but her knees were shaking and her voice quivered as she left her office. She managed a weak smile as she entered the meeting room twenty minutes later.

"Dr. Jankowski," Newton asked, after introducing her to those she didn't know, "when you went back through the Smith records, and your recollections of her labor and delivery, did you or can you see anything at all out of line that might have any bearing on the cause of this baby's deterioration to full-blown CP?"

"Clark, please call me Janet." *This is even worse than I imagined*, Janet thought to herself. "No, they seemed to be a textbook perfect couple for pregnancy, well-educated and healthy, with all the benefits of a good socioeconomic status, and Mrs. Smith had an uneventful pregnancy. I guess that's the problem; no one expected any difficulty. Very few parents can handle having a baby with CP, especially one as bad as this one is. This couple is no different than most."

Her voice grew stronger. "From the beginning of her pregnancy, both of them said that they couldn't tolerate a baby that wasn't normal. Because of her age, they were eager for amniocentesis and ultrasound, and they wanted a termination if anything abnormal was found. Both tests were normal."

Newton and the staff went through all the details to refresh everyone's memory. Janet commented once or twice, but she agreed with the summary.

"The only thing at all out of the ordinary I could find, throughout all of her care, was the loss of fetal heart-rate beat-to-beat variability from the time she came into the hospital in labor." Janet paused a moment to catch her breath. "I figured that the baby was probably just in a sleep cycle. Also, I was using an external monitor, which isn't as accurate as an internal one."

Newton nodded that he understood.

"After that, I thought perhaps it was the epidural anesthesia, which she insisted on having right away," she continued. "By that time, an internal monitor was attached. The first drop in heart tones, by itself, wasn't that abnormal, and the baby's heart rate returned to normal promptly, so we all agreed to wait. We see this happen every once in awhile, and almost always, nothing else happens out of the ordinary and the baby turns out fine. There really wasn't any problem with her anesthesia that I know of, either."

"We don't think so either," one of the committee members commented.

"When the heart tones went down the second time, I took her to a cesarean section about as fast as it's possible to go." Janet leaned forward. "I had maternal-fetal consultation during her labor, on the way to the c-section, and again afterwards, and all agreed we did things correctly. The biggest problem is that bastard, pardon me, George Thomas, who told the Smiths the next day that I had delayed. He talked to them very early in the morning, before I had a chance to make rounds, and even wrote it in the records that it was my fault and that he had told them about it. If it weren't for him, I really don't think this claim would have been made. That's all I know." Janet slumped back in her chair, exhausted.

"Well, everyone here agrees with you," Newton said. "We should have a unified front, except for Thomas. I'm certain you know Kim Workman in maternal-fetal medicine at the university. We're planning to use her as one of our experts."

"Sure. She's super." Janet actually smiled. "We've known each other since medical school, and we're good friends. I know she'll be glad to help. Tell me what I have to do now."

"Nothing right now, except to keep us informed of any developments. Again, any and all communication should go through us. Okay?" Newton looked squarely at her.

"Absolutely. May I talk with Kim? Actually, I have already," Janet confessed.

"Yes, that's a good idea, but you must not discuss this case with anyone else without our permission, except your husband, of course, and he shouldn't talk with anyone else either. I'm not trying to be insulting, but it's important that we keep talk and rumors at a minimum. We don't want Thomas, or anyone else, to know what we plan on doing."

"No problem," said Janet.

"Thanks for meeting with us, Janet. You're welcome to join us whenever you're free. Actually, it's probably a good idea for you to be here as often as you can to help with the details. We'll be talking about the Smith case at all our meetings for the next several weeks. We'll meet every Friday afternoon at the same time. It will be two to three hours each time, just like today."

"I'll be here," she answered grimly.

Newton began to collect his files from the table.

"Before we break, I want to let you know that I had a long talk with Chester House, the new attorney at University Hospital. He wants to be involved, and he will be there for your deposition, Janet, as well as for Workman's and for Thomas's, assuming a suit is actually filed. Neither of us can figure out why Kline hasn't involved the university maternal-fetal people so far. However, all of their attention seems to be directed toward you, Janet. That's a mistake, the first of many, we hope."

"It sure feels that way to me," Janet answered wryly.

"Secondly, House is as upset by Thomas as we are, so he wants to know first-hand what Thomas has to say. The excuse for involving House, unofficially, will be that you have privileges at University Hospital and that Workman and Thomas are university employees. I think he'll be a big help. I hope all agree?" Newton chatted with Janet and each of the members as they left.

After the meeting, Janet dragged herself through rounds, which took extra effort, given her exhaustion, and then returned to her office to call Kim.

"Hi. This is Janet. You're looking at the Smith case for me, I hear."

"Yes, that's right, and Janet, I don't think you did anything wrong, as I've told you repeatedly. In fact, from what I've seen so far of these records, you did everything right. I'll work on them more this weekend, but I don't think I'll find anything to make me change my opinion," Kim answered.

"Kim, thanks. I needed a little boost after the risk-management meeting this afternoon. Actually, it wasn't that bad, but I'm really depressed by the whole thing." She told Kim about the meeting. "Call me this weekend if you want me to clarify anything for you."

"I will. Let's plan to talk again next week. I'll be free as much as you need me to be. Don't give up, Janet."

Janet spent thirty minutes correcting and signing dictation, reading mail, and dictating responses. The enthusiasm she received from talking to Kim was quickly dispelled. Finally, she gathered herself together and made the drive home.

At home, Carol and Michael buoyed her spirits, briefly, with their chatter and enthusiasm about school and their weekend plans. Without promising, she considered joining them for a movie.

Later that evening, Janet described the meeting to Mike.

"They mean well, and they are on my side, but it sure is a funny feeling to sit there with people from other specialties who are judging care they really don't know all that much about. They'll get expert advice, and by the time it's all over, they'll probably know more about pregnancy, labor, and delivery than they want to know. I'm pretty certain they'll still agree with me then, but it sure hurts now. I talked with Kim afterward. The good news is that she'll be one of our expert witnesses."

When Mike tried to talk about his day, she interrupted.

"I'm sorry, Mike, but I need to go to bed. I'm exhausted." She gave him a peck on the cheek.

"I'll be up in a while," he called after her.

Janet didn't sleep very well again that night, one of many sleepless nights that she would have. She played and replayed her care of Angie Smith, always ending at one of the same two thoughts: either there were no changes she could find to make in the care she had given, or she had made a big mistake.

As the weekend progressed, her temper flared, and she rarely smiled. She snapped at the kids, refusing to play games. Mike finally took them to a movie to avoid a real blowup, while Janet spent most of the day in the study reading journal articles Newton had given her.

By Monday, Janet's sleeplessness and lack of appetite made her look even more drawn. Her despair was far worse than she was able to communicate.

"Mike, I'm still exhausted," she complained that morning at breakfast. "I didn't sleep more than thirty minutes at a time all weekend. Fortunately, I didn't have a delivery. I'm surprised I didn't wake you." He mumbled something inaudible. "These lawyers are really doing a number on my head, and I haven't even met with them yet. I've never been so upset."

Janet was so slow-moving that she was late arriving at the office. Her mood plummeted further when her first patient that morning asked her if she had been sick. Another one asked if something was wrong when she appeared to be daydreaming.

Janet curtailed her schedule to allow Friday afternoons for the meetings and another half-day each week for reading articles and documents. With Wednesday afternoon off for Kim and time for surgery, she was in the office less than three days a week.

Nancy asked her about night call.

"I guess I'll have to arrange coverage each Thursday night, so I can try to be rested for the meetings. I'll need even more time off as things develop, I'm afraid."

"Do you want me to tell patients who are due now?" Nancy asked.

"I guess so. Certainly, if they ask."

"What about referrals and old patients coming back?"

"Fit them into the time slots I have left. After that, I suppose we'll have to refer them elsewhere. I can use Wednesday afternoons for some of the reading for now, but I really want to keep up lunch with Kim." Janet sat back, already feeling defeated.

"I'll get things fixed. Now go to room two," Nancy said soothingly.

Kline asked Angie and Bill to come to his office for a conference about progress. Even he noticed how pale and haggard Angie appeared.

"I've talked with Dr. Thomas, and he is even more forceful than ever that there was a delay and that the delay caused the CP. I need an obstetrician on our side to support that position, so I'm going to talk with the maternal-fetal medicine person at Cloud View Hospital, Dr. Joseph Segal, to get his opinion. However, Thomas assures me that Segal will support us."

Angie stared at the desk. Bill nodded assent.

"Assuming that's true, we'll be ready to formally file the lawsuit. We'll have to list our experts soon after that, and we'll ask the defense to do the same. Once their experts are known, we must take depositions from them to see what their defense will be. They'll do the same with ours. We'll get the depositions going as quickly as we can to hurry this up. I know you're both anxious to put this behind you."

"We're more than anxious," Bill answered quietly, but firmly.

"This has ruined our lives," Angie exclaimed. "I'm too depressed to go see the baby anymore. He isn't getting any better." She burst into tears and clutched Bill's hand.

"Angie's right. This is tearing us both apart. We need to get the legal proceedings over with as soon as possible so we can get our lives in order and make plans for the future."

"Try to be patient." Kline spent several minutes reviewing the facts, allegations, and plans concerning the case. "I'll do the best I can to move this proceeding along. I think I've already told you that this sort of case usually takes years rather than months. We're doing quite well," answered Kline, as he showed them to the door. After Angie and Bill left, Kline looked into Jones's office and found him free.

"Jefferson, I'm going to talk to Dr. Segal this afternoon. He's free at two o'clock and has already reviewed the records. The Smiths want to push this as hard and fast as they can. They seem to think that winning this claim will solve all of their problems. I rather doubt that, but who am I to be a marriage or family counselor. I'll let you know what happens."

"Herb, are you still certain about this case? Remember what Pete Wilson said."

"We have no reason to think that Pete's one hundred percent right. Even he expressed some doubt. If Segal supports Thomas, it seems to me that we have a solid case. I've looked at it from all the angles I can think of, and I really don't expect any surprises down the road."

"I hope you're right, because it's a big investment of time if it doesn't work out."

"Remember, we have the retainer."

Kline had never met Joseph Segal before and was somewhat surprised to find that he was a short, bristling little man who dressed in very proper English clothes. Segal was a native of New York and had done all of his training in the northeast. He moved to St. Louis several years after his fellowship and promptly began to help plaintiff attorneys with bad baby cases. His motivation was strictly mercenary.

"Have you looked through the records?" Kline asked him.

Segal nodded, and they talked at length about the details.

"I think Dr. Thomas is dead right," Segal stated two hours later. "There was a clear delay by Dr. Jankowski, which is unquestionably the cause of the cerebral palsy in this baby. This is an open-and-shut case."

"Dr. Segal, others have noted the poor variability in this baby's heart rate from the time the monitor was put on, right after Mrs. Smith's admission to the hospital. What do you think about that?"

"It's there, but I don't think it's all that striking." He explained his opinion in some detail. "I'll stake my reputation on it."

"Well, you certainly are clear in your opinions. Thanks very much for your time. I look forward to working with you."

Kline drove to his office, feeling on top of the world.

"Jefferson, I just met with Segal, and both he and Thomas are certain that Dr. Jankowski delayed and that her delay was the cause of the CP in this baby. I can't get either of them to bend in the slightest. In fact, Segal says that he'll stake his reputation, whatever that is, on it. I think they'll be very convincing. My review of similar cases and of the medical literature supports this, so I think we're ready to start scheduling depositions. By the way, Segal charges even more than Thomas. I'll formally file the lawsuit and talk with Newton to get things going. Any problems?" Kline asked.

"No, I guess not. Just remember what Pete said. I know he doesn't like either Thomas or Segal, but I don't think that sways him in either direction. There's so much money involved that I guess we have to do it."

"Speaking of that, I'm going to have to ask the Smiths for more money."

"That's probably a good idea."

"Jefferson, how much do you think we should ask for from Dr. Jankowski? I've been thinking twenty million dollars."

"Herb, there hasn't been a judgment that large in this state for any medical malpractice case I know of."

"I know it, but this baby is really terribly damaged, the worst I've seen or heard of. I went by the NICU yesterday. His chances for recovery are nil, from what I could find out, and he will certainly be profoundly retarded. I realize we may not recover twenty million, but it's unlikely that a judge or jury will increase an award beyond our asking amount. That rarely happens."

"That's true. Go ahead at twenty million dollars."

"I'll call the Smiths now to let them know where we are." Kline went back to his office and phoned Angie.

"Mrs. Smith, we're ready to formally file the lawsuit and to begin depositions. Our experts agree that there was significant delay and that the delay caused the CP. Is there anything you or

Mr. Smith have left out about your pregnancy or labor, anything at all that could even remotely have bearing on the outcome?"

"No, nothing at all."

"Good. I'll get things scheduled as soon as I can. You and Mr. Smith will have to grant depositions to the defense. Clark Newton will ask you many of the same questions I've asked you, except he'll be much more forceful about it. That's his job. Mr. Jones and I will be there to keep things on track. Oh, yes, and we'll need another ten thousand dollars from you toward expenses for our experts. I hope that's okay?"

"I'm sure we can manage," Angie answered. "By the way, I'm going to go back to work part time, starting next week. Wilma will be here when I come home each day."

"It might be a good idea to depose Wilma, too. She would be a good witness to the mental turmoil and stress you've been through. Suggest it to her, please."

"I'm sure she will agree."

"The asking amount in the lawsuit will be twenty million dollars. We think that's as high as we can reasonably go. Is that okay?"

"Yes. Certainly. I know Bill will agree."

"Thank you."

11

Clark Newton and Kim Workman settled themselves at his conference table.

"Good morning, Kim. I hope you've had a chance to go through the records on the Smith case."

"Clark, I've been through these records several times. I don't think there was any delay, and that's not just because some of my people were consultants or because Janet trained at the university and is my friend. There just wasn't a delay. That moronic, money-grubbing George Thomas is the one at fault for telling the Smiths that there was. To make it worse, he wrote it in both the mother's and the baby's charts. And then he got the plaintiff attorneys to use his friend, Joseph Segal. I wish there were something we could do about those two." Her face was rigid.

"So do I. They're becoming annoying," Newton responded.

"Janet and I have been meeting for lunch for years. I'm sure she told you that we're friends. As you might imagine, we've talked extensively about Mrs. Smith's care, ever since the delivery. Her description of what happened, and why, makes me even more convinced that there was no negligence. Incidentally, Janet looks terrible. This is destroying her. She used to be such a confident, happy person."

"I understand your anger, Kim, but that won't help us win this case. And I'm sorry to hear about Janet. I guess I suspected she wasn't taking it very well. But what do you make of the lack of beat-to-beat variability when this mother came in, before anything was done? Both the plaintiff experts say it's nothing," Newton asked.

"I'm not surprised, because they're both too dumb or too greedy to pay attention. Probably, it's both. The puzzling part about both of them is that they were trained in good institutions, and Thomas, at least, is a good doctor. I don't know Segal well enough to comment. I guess money just became more important to them. I think the lack of variability is the key to our defense. Let me try to explain," Kim said.

"Please do," Newton responded eagerly.

"As you know, we don't know what causes cerebral palsy. In fact, we aren't even sure we know exactly what it is, except for the spastic paralysis or palsy most of these babies have. Beyond that, there can be wide variation, some of them being normally intelligent to brilliant, and some being retarded. It would look as if this baby will be profoundly retarded, I'm afraid," Kim explained.

"That makes it much tougher for us," Newton observed.

"When fetal monitoring came along in the late sixties and early seventies, we thought we would be able to pinpoint the events that caused CP, and we thought that they occurred during labor and delivery. We hoped to actually prevent CP. Unfortunately, that just hasn't been the case. The incidence of CP has not changed appreciably since World War II, in spite all the newfangled monitoring and tests we've developed. Two or three babies out of a thousand will get CP, and that may rise a little as NICUs are able to keep very small babies alive."

"What should we do to prove our case?" Newton asked.

"I'm not sure. How much workup have they done on this baby? I couldn't find the results of a CT scan on the brain, which should be routine. There should also be a test for cytomegalovirus," Kim said.

"Neither's been done," Newton answered. "It looks like Thomas is avoiding tests that might jeopardize his case, or he didn't even think of them. He'll certainly use the excuse that they're not needed. I'll suggest that both be done. Fortunately, the plaintiff attorney, Herbert Kline, is greedy, besides being tough. If I present this right, he'll think it'll help his case, and he'll convince his clients. What do you think?"

"Clark, I know this is supposed to be the perfect couple and the perfect marriage, but they do live in a world where alcohol, drugs, and other mood altering substances are common. If anything happened to the baby at let's say seven months of pregnancy, it might show up now on a CT scan of the brain. CMV can also cause CP or something like it, so we need to look there, too. We can't count on anything, but it would help if something's there."

"Kim, did you look at the anesthesia records enough to rule out problems there?"

"I don't think anything happened with the anesthesia. To be sure, you should talk to the anesthesiologists directly."

"I will, as soon as I can." Newton wrote himself a note.

"Good, and I'll keep working on a medical literature search to find information to support us."

Newton called Kline.

"Herb, I notice that there isn't a CT scan of the baby's brain on record. Also, no cytomegalovirus test has been done. It might be helpful to us both if we know for certain that the baby doesn't have any internal brain damage. Will you try to get the parents' permission and take care of it?"

"I'm surprised," Kline answered. "Thomas has testified previously that CT scans of the brain are routine in this type of case. Consider both done. By the way, we formally filed this morning. There should be a message with your office staff to that effect."

"I thought you would be doing that soon. Thanks for telling me."

"Mrs. Smith, it's Mr. Kline on line two."

"Thanks." She picked up the phone.

"Hello, Mr. Kline."

"Mrs. Smith, we need to get a CT scan of the baby's brain. I'm sure that it will be normal and that it will improve our case against Dr. Jankowski. They're also going to do a test for cytomegalovirus. You'll need to go to the hospital to sign the permission papers for the CT," Kline directed her.

"If you insist. I'm sure I can do it this afternoon when I'm there." Her voice was monotone, and she promptly hung up.

"I'll count on it," Kline said, irritated by the disconnect.

"Dr. Thomas, this is Herb Kline." He was surprised to get through right away. "Mrs. Smith is coming over to sign a permission slip for a CT scan of her baby's brain. I'm sure you'll agree, since you're on record that they should be routine on any baby with apparent brain damage."

"Oh, okay. But I don't see any purpose here; the case is so cut-and-dry. It's just one more expense that will have no value to us," Thomas responded. "I'll write the order for the CT when Mrs. Smith comes by. Since it's not an emergency, it may take a couple of weeks to get it done."

"That's fine. Also, get a CMV test. That should be routine, too. Thank you."

House also talked to Kim at some length about the Smith case. He and Kim agreed to work together, as she was to do with Newton, and he told her he would be at Thomas's and her depositions, as well as Janet's.

"I'm glad you're involved. Maybe we can do something about Thomas once and for all. Call me anytime, Mr. House."

"I will."

Before Newton could call Janet, she was on the phone to him, in a panic.

"Clark, a deputy sheriff served me with a subpoena about twenty minutes ago. He just marched into my waiting room and upset all my patients and my staff. I had to stop everything while he formally handed it to me and made me sign for it. Why didn't you warn me?"

"I'm sorry, Janet. Kline, typically, doesn't tell me ahead of time, but I did forget to tell you that the deputy sheriff is routine."

"It made me feel like a criminal. At least there's no more suspense, I guess."

"That's true, Janet, but now we worry about the outcome. Did you read enough of the subpoena to know that they're asking for twenty million dollars in actual and punitive damages?"

"Oh, my God. I've never heard of a suit that high" Her heart began to pound again, and she collapsed into her chair, which, fortunately, was right behind her. She hadn't read the subpoena completely, thinking it was just routine.

"It's one of the highest in a medical malpractice case, at least in this area. So far, there hasn't been a judgment even close to that amount."

"I can't believe this. What comes next?" Janet was still gasping for breath, and she felt flushed and uneasy.

"We're asking Thomas to order a CT scan of the baby's brain. It should be done in a couple of weeks."

"Why do you want to do that?" Janet asked.

"Actually, it's Kim's idea. Some of the mood-altering substances popular right now can damage the fetal brain, causing problems just like CP. Also, there could be a congenital defect. The CT should have been routine in the workup of the baby. We're also getting a CMV test done. That's another couple of mistakes on their side."

"I didn't have any reason to think that either of the Smiths used drugs. Did I miss something?" Janet asked.

"I don't think so, but Kim feels that we should do it. Most of all, she's hoping for a congenital defect; as she said, many in the Smiths's social set do use drugs. Did you do any urine screening?"

"No. As you know, in Missouri we have to have the patient's permission to screen for drugs, and I didn't have any reason to think she used them."

"Well, I just wanted you to know what we were doing."

"Okay." Janet was not reassured.

"I'll call you if anything changes. See you at the next committee meeting."

Janet promptly called Mike. She remained seated, her heart still racing, but she had better control of her breathing and could talk coherently when he finally came to the phone.

"Mike, it's happened."

"What's happened, honey?"

"The Smith lawsuit against me and Memorial was formally filed today, for twenty million dollars." She related the whole story to him.

"Oh, Janet, I'm so sorry. I hoped they would drop it. I guess that was unrealistic, especially now that we know how much money they're trying to get."

"Newton says it's the highest amount he's heard of around here for this kind of case."

"Janet, they can't possibly hope to get that much. Maybe they think they can scare you and Newton into a settlement. If that's the case, I know they're wrong."

"That's for sure. Now the depositions will start. God, I'm not sure I'm ready for them."

"You'll do fine, honey. I know it. I love you."

"I love you too, Mike. Thanks. I'll see you this evening."

Janet hung up and fell back into her chair, wanting to

scream in anger and in desperation. She waved to Nancy to close the door, then stared blankly at the wall.

Her head felt as if it would explode, and she realized that her blood pressure had to be sky high. By breathing slowly and deeply, her head became numb and all thoughts seemed to stop. Finally, she felt as if she were tumbling into a dark hole, with no chance of getting out. She began to cry, quietly at first, but soon, she was sobbing.

Nancy brought her a glass of water and a cold towel, which helped a little, but the final reality of the lawsuit and its magnitude were more than she could manage. She knew she wasn't behaving well, but she couldn't help herself.

Reluctantly, Janet explained the lawsuit to her office staff and went home early, having Nancy reschedule the rest of her patients. Her sadness overwhelmed her, and she even had some difficulty negotiating the drive home, taking twice as long as usual. Once there, she curled up on her bed and continued to cry off and on throughout the rest of the afternoon.

The children seemed quite upset when they came home from school. Janet wouldn't let them in even to say hello, so they waited by the window, watching the driveway, and threw themselves on Mike when he came in.

"Kids, kids, what's the matter?"

"Mom's upstairs, crying," Michael shouted.

"Come on, let's go see her."

"Hi, guys." Janet tried to smile through her tear-stained face when they walked into the bedroom together. "I guess I'm being a baby. Sorry."

"What's the matter, Mom?" they demanded to know.

"Kids, it's the same old thing. Problems at work. Why don't you go downstairs. I'll be there in a few minutes, and I'll try to explain then."

"Go on, kids. I'll be right there," Mike directed them. "Are you okay?" he asked after they were gone.

"Yes, I'm okay. I just decided to have a good cry. I'll be right down."

Mike left to tend to the children.

Janet washed her face, combed her hair, and went down to dinner, although she ate next to nothing. She and Mike tried to explain about the lawsuit, which both children seemed to understand a little from watching TV. Finally, they all talked about how school had been that day. Janet didn't want the lawsuit to upset them anymore than it already had.

After the children were in bed, Janet turned to Mike.

"Come here, and just hold me. Maybe I can stop wanting to cry for a while. This is so devastating that I don't know what to do."

She told him what had happened at the office after she had called him. As always, he told her that she would survive the lawsuit and that he was absolutely sure she hadn't done anything wrong. She gradually began to relax, and they went to bed, where he held her until she finally fell asleep from exhaustion.

Notice of the lawsuit against Janet and Memorial Hospital was published two days later on the front page of the second section of the morning newspaper. The article spelled out, in detail, the allegations made, and it contained no rebuttal by either Newton or Janet. In fact, they had not even been contacted. The headline read: LOCAL DOCTOR CHARGED FOR BAD BABY. The article was brief and unsympathetic to Janet. It highlighted the request for twenty million dollars.

There were also short announcements on two of the three local TV channels, both occurring in the morning, according to reports from patients. One even said that Dr. Jankowski had not been available for comment, although no attempt had been made to reach her or the hospital.

Janet was overwhelmed when she heard about the TV spot from a patient. In tears again, she called Newton, trying to choke back her sobs.

"What do I do? This will ruin me. It's so damn unfair," she cried out.

"Janet, this sort of thing is routine. Unfortunately, they won't report or print any rebuttal from me, so I don't even try. I'm sorry I didn't tell you to expect this, but I guess I assumed you had seen similar notices about other doctors from time to time."

"I guess I have. That's partly what's so upsetting. I believed some of those articles and TV reports about other doctors, and I'm sure everyone believes now that I'm responsible for a bad baby."

"I think you'll be surprised at how little is seen or remembered. I'll bet you can't even remember the names of the other doctors, let alone any of the details surrounding their specific cases."

"Clark, I hope you're right."

She hung up and called Mike, after which she regained control and finished seeing her patients. She has always thought of herself as professional, and she didn't want to let her patients down; she already had to reschedule the patients from the previous afternoon.

The idea of telling her parents about the official filing of the lawsuit and the newspaper and TV notices was especially disturbing to her. However, she pulled herself together and made the call. Both her mother and father were supportive, telling her to ignore the media and to go on practicing the best she knew how. Both of them said they were certain she would win the case.

When she was finally able to leave the office and was finished with hospital rounds, her stomach lurched and burned all the way home. She was much less certain about the outcome than her parents or Mike were.

"Mike, I went to the University NICU last night after my

delivery. I've done that a couple of other times before."

"Why do you take the time then, instead of coming home to bed? You sure need the sleep."

"I guess I don't want to see Thomas or the Smiths. Anyhow, the baby looks terrible. The nurses have to clear his nose and throat all the time because he can't swallow, and he isn't getting any better."

"It doesn't sound good, Janet."

"Honey, I don't see how I can possibly win this case with the way he looks. Thank God, we were fortunate to have two normal babies."

"Amen to that. However, I think you're being too pessimistic about the lawsuit. Newton and Kim both think that you'll come through with flying colors."

"I sure hope they're right."

Janet went to bed early, hoping that sleep would combat her exhaustion. But her dreams began to change. She awakened several times that night, and many times after that, dripping wet and very frightened. In the morning, she remembered only darkness and noise, as if she had been in the middle of a violent storm. Unseen and unidentified, but very frightening, threats came from all directions. There seemed to be loud noises like thunder or worse. Her mind was in complete turmoil. She often woke up screaming.

She and Mike talked a lot about her mood and her sleeplessness, and both agreed that she shouldn't use a sleeping pill, afraid of the aftereffects, especially if she had to get up for a delivery. They seriously considered a counselor, but Janet refused. Nevertheless, the nightmares were so upsetting that Janet was almost afraid to go to bed. Her skin became sallow and her cheeks hollow.

12

Kline and Jones planned their strategy amidst some minor disagreements.

"I know we've filed the lawsuit and that we're about to begin our first deposition, but something about this case keeps nagging at me," Jones observed. "I guess it's Pete Wilson's hesitancy, but there's something else that I just can't grasp. On top of that, things are going too smoothly." He shook his head.

"Too smoothly?" asked Kline.

"Usually, by this time, we've uncovered problems, even if they're minor. I haven't seen any problems yet, and that, combined with the eagerness of Thomas and Segal, is a little unsettling. This is the first time we haven't had any trouble scheduling any of our experts, or theirs, for deposition." Jones looked up at his partner.

"I know. It bothers me, too," Kline answered, nodding in agreement. "We've got a lot at stake here, so we'll just have to be extra careful. I went through all the details again last night. I'm sure you did, too. Except for Pete's concern, which I think is minor, I'm certain we have a solid case. However, Newton's very thorough, so we want to be on top of everything. Let's keep going over this together every day as if it's a brand new claim, just to make sure."

"I agree." Jones nodded. "Also, I suggest you try to keep Newton under control during Angie Smith's deposition. She's really fragile, and we can't afford to have her break down. Who knows what she'd say, then."

"Good idea," Kline said. Their secretary announced that everyone was ready.

Kline ushered the Smiths and Newton into their conference room, which was also the office library. The walls were covered with walnut bookcases, which were filled with leather-bound law books and bound case records. The center table was made of polished black marble, and the chairs were covered with dark leather. Bill and Angie sat together on one side, Jones and Kline sat on the other side, and Newton sat at the head. The court reporter was already seated in a corner with her stenographer's machine. She had also set up a tape recorder in the middle of the table, and she asked each of them to spell their names.

Angie and Bill were dressed in sober business suits, dark gray for him and navy for her. The lawyers, in marked contrast to the quiet, almost somber, Smiths, were in their customary attire and were jovial and friendly with each other.

"Mr. and Mrs. Smith, since this is your first deposition, I'd like to explain some things to you," Kline announced. "First, this is Clark Newton, who is the attorney for Memorial Hospital and for Dr. Janet Jankowski." They shook hands. "He will begin the deposition, and he will be doing most of the questioning this morning. His purpose is to find out all the facts surrounding your allegations against Memorial Hospital and Dr. Jankowski. That's why this is called a discovery deposition. We will have the same opportunity with each of their witnesses, including Dr. Jankowski."

He paused to be sure there were no questions.

"The first of you to be deposed this morning will be Mrs. Smith, followed by Mr. Smith. Mr. Jones and I will be here to raise objections or to clarify issues if there are any problems. We may ask each of you a few questions at the end, also. Do you understand the procedure?"

"Yes," said Angie and Bill.

"This is the court reporter who will swear you in and record everything," Kline added. "Let's begin."

"Do you swear to tell the truth, the whole truth, and nothing but the truth?" asked the court reporter.

"I do," answered Angie. She seemed to be calm and controlled.

"State your full name, please," said Newton.

"Angela Wilson Smith."

"Are you a resident of this city?"

"Yes, in Ladue."

"How long have you lived here?"

"All my life."

"Did you go away to go to college?"

"No. I attended Washington University. I did live on campus."

"Did you graduate from Washington U?"

"Yes, I did."

"Are you employed?"

"Yes."

"By whom?"

"ZBL Computers."

"When did you begin work there?"

"In the fall after I graduated."

"Why not before then?"

"I spent the summer traveling in Europe with Bill on our honeymoon."

"What does ZBL stand for?"

"Zablonski, Bertram, and Lord. They are the founders of the company."

"What does ZBL Computers do?"

"We design or provide software programming and service to professional offices for accounting, scheduling, and other office management functions."

"Do you sell computers?"

"No. We may give advice about purchasing a computer, but we do not sell them directly."

"What is your position with ZBL Computers?"

"I work in the training section."

"What does the training section do?"

"We train new employees for the various design, programming, sales, and maintenance functions of the company."

Newton read from a list of questions, ticking off each one as she answered.

"Isn't it true that you are supposed to receive a promotion?"

"Yes."

"To what position?"

"Head of the training section."

"When is that supposed to occur?"

"As soon as I return to full-time status, if I do."

"What do you mean by if?"

"My delivery and the baby's condition have upset me so much that I can't do anything with any enthusiasm anymore."

"That doesn't answer my question. What do you mean by if?"

"It's a figure of speech. I'll go back to full time soon."

"Do you expect to be promoted?"

"I think so."

"Is your job in jeopardy?"

"No, I don't think so."

"Have they, ZBL Computers, given you any deadline for response?"

"No, although I'm sure I'll need to let them know soon."

"Was your son, William N. Smith, Jr., born at Memorial Hospital on December 8, 1992?"

This was one of the questions she dreaded, and it showed in her face. "Yes."

"Is it true that the delivery was done by cesarean section, as an emergency?"

"Yes."

"Was this delivery at full term?"

"Yes."

"Was this your first pregnancy?"

"Yes."

"State your age please."

"Thirty-seven."

"Dr. Janet Jankowski was your doctor?"

"Yes."

"Did you see any other physician during your pregnancy?"

"No, not until I went into the hospital."

"Didn't you have genetic counseling and testing at the University Hospital early in your pregnancy?"

"Yes. I thought you were asking if I saw another obstetrician for prenatal care."

"Isn't it true that you saw the genetics and maternal-fetal doctors at University Hospital on several occasions and that you also saw a radiologist and maternal-fetal specialist who did ultrasound exams on you?"

"That's really two questions," Kline interrupted, "but I'll let it go this time. Answer both please, Mrs. Smith."

"Yes to both questions."

"Were those genetic and ultrasound exams normal?" Newton resumed.

"That's what I was told."

"We will stipulate that all of her exams and tests were normal," interjected Kline.

Newton dug in harder.

"Was there any hint of anything abnormal during your pregnancy?"

"Not that I was told of."

"Are you suggesting that something was hidden from you or your husband?"

"No."

"Then please answer the question directly."

"The exams were normal, and there was no hint of anything wrong." Angie spoke very distinctly and slowly, biting off her words.

"Was anything wrong with you or your pregnancy that you know of when you came to the hospital in labor?"

"No."

"When were you first aware that perhaps something was not going right?"

"Late in my labor, when I was about six centimeters dilated, there was a big slow-down in the baby's heart rate, which I saw and heard on the monitor. Bill was there, too."

"Was Dr. Jankowski there?"

"Yes."

"Was she there throughout the entire labor?"

"Yes."

"So she was paying attention during your labor?"

"Yes," Angie answered grudgingly.

Kline choked. Jones put his hand on Kline's arm, looked him in the eye, and expressed surprise.

"What happened when the heart rate dropped at the time you described?" Newton asked.

"I don't understand your question."

"What did Dr. Jankowski or the nurses do?"

"They turned me on my left side, increased the IV fluids, and gave me oxygen through my nose. I guess that's all."

"What happened to the heart rate?"

"It came back up after a bit."

"Isn't it true that it went back to normal?"

"Yes."

"Then what happened?"

"The heart rate stayed normal for about thirty minutes and then dropped again."

"Was Dr. Jankowski there for the entire thirty minutes?"

"Yes."

"In the room?"

"Yes, either in the room or right outside."

"What happened when it went down the second time?"

"They rushed me in for a cesarean section."

"By they, do you mean Dr. Jankowski?"

"Yes." A tear crept from Angie's right eye. She quickly brushed it away.

"How long was it before the baby was born?"

"They put me to sleep, so I don't know for sure, but they told me it that it was seventeen minutes."

"From the time the heart rate dropped?"

"Yes."

"You were asleep, so you didn't know how the baby was right away. When were you made aware that things were not okay?"

"Later that evening when Bill told me."

"What did he say?"

"About the baby?"

"Yes, about the baby."

"Bill said that the baby didn't cry right and that he was very floppy. He also said that they rushed the baby to the NICU at Memorial."

"Is that all he said?"

"That's enough."

"Bill is your husband? You mentioned him before."

"Of course."

"Please understand, Mrs. Smith, I'm not trying to be difficult, but the record must be clear to anyone who reads it. When did you first talk with a doctor about your baby?"

She paused for a couple of sips of water.

"Dr. Jankowski came by that evening and talked to Bill, but I don't remember much of it."

"So when did you talk to someone that you remember?"

"The next morning."

"Who was that?"

"Dr. Thomas."

"Do you mean Dr. George Thomas?"

"Yes."

"Was that before Dr. Jankowski talked to you again?"

"Yes. He came in very early."

"What did Dr. Thomas tell you?"

"He said that the baby wasn't normal."

"Is that all he said?"

"No."

"Go ahead and answer the question completely," Kline told his client.

"He said that it looked as if the baby had brain damage. He also said that there had been a long delay by Dr. Jankowski in reacting to the drop in heart tones."

"Did he say anything else?"

"He said that the baby would certainly have been normal if she hadn't delayed." Tears ran from both of her eyes.

"Are you sure that's what he said?"

Kline stepped in.

"You're badgering. She's answered the question."

"When did Dr. Jankowski see you?" Newton resumed questioning immediately.

"Later that morning."

"What time was it?"

"Just before eight o'clock."

"So, Dr. Thomas must have come in very early. What time was that?"

"Before seven o'clock, I think. I was still asleep."

"What did Dr. Jankowski do when she came in to see you?"

"She took off the dressing and looked at my incision. Then she asked if I was urinating and eating."

"Did she say or do anything else?"

"She listened to my chest and felt my uterus. She asked about bleeding. She said that the incision looked fine and that I could eat anything I wanted."

"Is that all she said? Didn't she mention the baby?"

"Yes. She said that she didn't know what had happened, that they had done things as quickly as was reasonable and possible, and that there wasn't anything wrong with the placenta or umbilical cord."

"Was that the only time she saw you?"

"No. She saw me each morning and evening until I went home."

"Did she say anything more about the baby or the delivery?"

"No. She told me to talk to the neonatologists, and she gave me discharge instructions."

"What's happened to the baby since then?"

Angie paused for several moments and drank some more water. Finally, she answered.

"He has CP and hasn't even come home from the hospital yet. I don't know if he'll ever come home."

"By CP, do you mean cerebral palsy?"

"Yes."

"Mrs. Smith, did you use drugs or alcohol during your pregnancy?"

"No. Never."

"Isn't it true that you had severe nausea and vomiting early on in the pregnancy?"

"Yes."

"Didn't you use any kind of medication then?"

"No. The doctor said there weren't any that were safe to take."

"So, you didn't take anything? How about prenatal vitamins?"

"Yes. I also took iron pills, but nothing else."

"You stated that your son hasn't come home yet. What is the reason for that?"

"He doesn't suck at all and doesn't swallow very well. About all he does is lie in the bassinet. If someone touches him, he goes into spasm and his legs and arms pull up even more."

"What do the doctors plan to do with him?"

"I'm not sure, but they're talking about taking out the feeding tube through his throat and putting one in through his tummy. I don't quite understand it all."

"Do they think your baby will get better?"

"I haven't been given a straight answer to that question."

"That's all," Newton said. "I have no more questions."

"I don't have any questions either," Kline responded.

"Nothing here." Jones concluded the deposition by calling for a fifteen-minute restroom break.

13

Bill relaxed some during the break, but he was still seething because Angie had been subjected to so many questions.

"How are you, honey?" he asked, leading her away from the others.

"I don't know. Numb more than anything. I'm glad it's over, that's for sure."

"I hope he doesn't go through the same things with me. It's a waste of time," Bill growled.

They reached the front door.

"Let's go outside. I need the fresh air," Angie said.

After a couple of minutes, they slowly walked back to the library.

"Mr. Smith, do you swear to tell the truth, the whole truth, and nothing but the truth?" the court reporter asked him.

"I do." Bill seemed very intense.

"Please state your full name," Newton said.

"William Nelson Smith."

"Are you a resident of this city?"

"Yes."

"How long have you lived here?"

"All my life."

"Did you go away to college?"

"No. I attended and graduated from Washington University. I lived on campus, too. Angie and I met there."

"How old are you?"

"Thirty-seven."

"How long have you and Mrs. Smith been married?"

"Sixteen years."

"Are you employed in this city?"

"Yes."

"Where are you employed?"

"ZBL Computers."

"Is it true that you are their sales manager?"

"Yes."

"How long have you been the sales manager?"

"Since November first, shortly before the baby was born."

"Did you have any suspicion that there was anything wrong with Mrs. Smith's pregnancy or with the baby?"

"That's two questions," Kline interrupted.

"Okay. The pregnancy first," Newton responded.

"No."

"Now the baby."

"Not until things went wrong during the labor."

"What happened after your son was born?"

"He was limp and had a funny cry."

"Did he seem to be normal otherwise?"

Kline spoke up again.

"We will stipulate that the baby was normal otherwise, meaning that it had no visible defects and that it has subsequently become obvious that he has cerebral palsy and possible severe retardation."

"Thank you. What did Dr. Jankowski say to you when it was apparent that something was wrong with the baby?" Newton continued his line of questioning.

"She didn't say much of anything. She seemed overwhelmed by things."

"She didn't say anything at all?"

"No, she did say that she didn't know what the problem was

and that the neonatologists would take care of the baby and keep us informed."

"Was this while she was finishing up the cesarean section?"

"Yes. Then I left when they took the baby to the NICU."

"Where did you go?"

"To the NICU. I could watch through the window."

"Were you there each time Dr. Jankowski came into Mrs. Smith's room after that?"

"Yes, I stayed in the hospital room with Angie. They put up a cot for me."

"Did she have a private room?"

"Yes. We requested one."

"What did Dr. Jankowski say on the other days when she came in, before Mrs. Smith went home?"

"She kept repeating the same thing, that she didn't know what went wrong or when it happened and that the neonatologists would take care of the baby."

"Did Dr. Jankowski say anything about the heart tones during labor?"

"Not very much. I had to ask her."

"What did she say?"

"She said that the lack of variability noticed at admission and during labor couldn't be explained easily, but that she thought that it was either a sleep cycle or the epidural."

"Did she say anything else?"

"We talked about the first drop in heart rate. She said that she was almost ready to do a cesarean section, but then the rate went back up to normal. When it happened again, they went immediately to a c-section."

"Anything else?"

"She did say that she had consulted with the maternal-fetal specialists right after the first drop began, and that they had agreed with her care."

"Was Dr. Jankowski there the whole time?"

"When?"

"During Mrs. Smith's labor."

"Yes. She was in Angie's room most of the time or right outside."

"So, she was aware of what was going on with the baby at all times?"

"Yes, she was." Bill became more deliberate.

"Did you talk to Dr. Thomas?"

"Yes. I was there when he came in the next morning."

"What did Dr. Thomas say?"

"Just what Angie said."

"Please tell us in your own words."

"He said that the baby had brain damage because of Dr. Jankowski's delay in responding to the drop in the heart rate."

"Is that all he said?"

"No. He said that the baby would probably develop CP."

"By CP, you mean cerebral palsy?"

"Yes, of course."

"Did he say anything else?"

"Then, or sometime, he said that the baby would be retarded, probably severely." Bill glared at Newton.

"Did Dr. Thomas come in to see you and your wife more than once?"

"He came in at least once each day."

"What did he say during those visits?"

"The same thing, that it was Dr. Jankowski's fault that our baby has CP and that he will most likely be severely retarded."

"Did you use drugs during this pregnancy?"

"No. Never."

"Alcohol?"

"Rarely, since Angie wasn't allowed to."

"That's all I have," said Newton.

"I have nothing," Kline answered.

"Nothing here either," Jones echoed.

"Angie and Bill, I think your depositions went very well. That's a tough process, and you were both great." Kline smiled at them. "The next steps will be depositions taken by Clark Newton from Dr. Thomas and from Dr. Segal, our maternal-fetal expert. We will also take a deposition from Dr. Jankowski soon. Newton will certainly have several experts on his side for us to depose. We do want to depose Wilma James, to have another witness to your mental anguish and the disruption of your home."

Angie nodded that she agreed.

"With luck, we can do one of these each week. By that time, we should have a pretty good idea of how things are going. We think we'll have it all wrapped up soon, and we should be able to demand a very satisfactory settlement. Do you have any questions?" Kline asked.

"I guess not," both of them answered, overwhelmed by all of his news. They were still angry and very tired, which was expected, since the depositions lasted over four hours.

"Then why don't you both go home and get some rest?"

Angie and Bill drove home in silence until, finally, she spoke.

"I'm sure glad that's done. I just wish they could get this whole thing over with more quickly." She snapped her words out.

"Actually, I think Kline is moving things along faster than usual. I don't know if that's because of a concern for us or because he smells a big fee when we win. I suspect it's the latter," Bill answered.

"I'm sure you're right, Bill."

They pulled up to the house. Bill walked Angie in, and she immediately began chattering with Wilma about the depositions. He excused himself and went to his office at ZBL, staying there until almost midnight to catch up. Angie didn't awaken when he came home. The next morning, she asked him what time he had come in, but he didn't respond to the question.

Newton called Janet at her office.

"The first two depositions with the Smiths went okay. It's clear that they are both becoming dysfunctional over this. She's got her emotions flattened to the point of being unresponsive. He's blustering as if he's afraid he won't complete a sale." He told her the details of each deposition, and he told her that he would give her copies. "Maybe you can pick them up tomorrow when you make rounds. What time do you come back to the hospital in the evening?"

"Probably at about five-thirty. I'll come to your office then."

"I should be here. Let me know if you'll be much later than that. Okay?"

"Sure."

Janet walked into his office the next day at five-forty, apologizing for her lateness.

"Don't worry about it," he said, handing her the stack of papers. "Go through them carefully, so you get a feel for what will happen with you. Thomas is scheduled next week. We'll talk more after that, and we'll go over everything at our Friday committee meeting each week."

"Thanks, Clark."

That evening, after dinner, when Carol and Michael were studying in their rooms, Janet repeated everything to Mike.

"The first two depositions with the Smiths are over. I wasn't there, but Newton called me, and now I have the copies of the depositions. I guess they went okay, except he feels that the Smiths are both falling apart. That could hurt if we ever go to trial.

I think it would make the jury more sympathetic to them."

"I don't know. That's a hard one to call." Mike realized that no one cared how much Janet's life, or his, were disrupted. Physicians were supposedly immune. They talked more after Carol and Michael were in bed, seeking quiet attempts at closeness, which failed.

Janet was becoming unraveled a little more each day. Her confidence about medicine was declining, and she questioned every action she took, even those that were routine. Nancy and Darlene fielded complaints from patients about appointments running late, and patient volume dropped.

"Dr. Johnson," Nancy called Mike, "Dr. Jankowski is having problems keeping up. In fact, she had one patient walk out before she was even seen this afternoon. That's the first time that's ever happened."

"How late was she?"

"Well over an hour, and that's routine now for most of her patients."

"What do you want to do?"

"Dr. Johnson, if it's okay with you, Darlene and I would like to schedule her appointments further apart, without telling her. She hasn't looked at the appointment book in weeks. I think we can keep people happier that way, if we can get her to start on time instead of her just sitting in her chair, staring vacantly at the walls."

"I'm sorry to hear about the problems. Spreading out the appointment times sounds good to me. Call me whenever you want."

"Janet, what can I do to help you out of this depression?" Mike asked her that evening. "You can't keep on like this."

"Mike, I don't know. This is absolute agony. I've tried everything I can think of. I find myself sitting in the office between patients, just staring into space, sometimes for five to ten minutes. I feel so empty. Nancy is beginning to check on me to keep the schedule from falling even further behind."

"Are you seeing any drop-off in new patients?"

"No, I don't think so. Actually, I really don't know," she answered.

"Well, it ought to make you feel good that your referring doctors still like you enough to keep sending patients."

"I know, but I'm finding that I don't enjoy talking with the new ones like I used to. I worry that one of them will be another lawsuit. I know it's crazy, but I can't help it. This thing is really getting to me."

"I'm sorry, honey," he repeated, as he had so many times before. Mike knew that the number of new patients would drop because Nancy's call about spacing appointment times would make the waiting period to get in even longer. Once it stayed beyond nine or ten weeks, a significant drop-off would occur. Janet's practice was definitely in trouble.

Mike was more than a little ambivalent about the changes he had okayed. In the long run, they were what he wanted—for her to be less busy and home more—but he hated the surreptitious way he was making it happen. Sooner or later, he knew he would have to account for his interference.

Nights were a battleground of thunder and noise for Janet. She dreaded going to sleep, but she was exhausted to the point of falling asleep while sitting and even standing. She frequently found herself waving her arms when she awakened during the night, as if trying to protect herself.

Janet's heart raced, and she gasped for breath. Her sleep was never longer that three or four hours a night, in segments of thirty minutes or less. She was angry at the Smiths, the lawyers, and the system, and she was angry at herself for not handling things better. She knew the children were being affected, and that made her despair even deeper.

Janet's father tried to console her by putting most of the blame on the Smiths.

"They are at fault for not being able to accept that bad outcomes are inevitable once in a while, and that it does not mean that you or anyone else has done something wrong. Janet, you've got to accept that also."

"But Daddy, this baby is just awful."

"I know it. But that still doesn't make it your fault. Just put it behind you."

Janet knew her father was trying to help. "But I can't help feeling there's something I could have done," she cried to herself. She didn't phone her parents anymore and didn't notice that they didn't call her either. Another comfortable routine was disrupted.

Janet gave up all pretense of family activities, letting Mike carry the load. The word "fun" was gone from her vocabulary. Instead, she spent each evening and weekend, when not delivering a baby, brooding about the Smith case, sitting in the study with stacks of textbooks, journal articles, and depositions. Occasionally she read a little and made notes. Usually, she stared blankly at the floor or wall.

14

"Dr. Thomas, I believe you know Clark Newton and my partner, Jefferson Jones," Kline said. They met in Thomas's office, at his insistence.

"Yes, I've met both. Good morning," he responded coldly.

"This is Chester House, who is the new university attorney. I don't think you've met him."

Thomas shook hands with him perfunctorily.

House tried to engage Thomas in pleasantries, but failed.

"I'll be present for both Dr. Workman's and your depositions, since you are both university employees. I hope that will be okay?" House asked.

Thomas nodded.

"Is he going to participate?" Kline asked. "If so, he must be listed in the formal documents as a member of the defense team."

"No, he won't be involved in any direct or rebuttal questioning, but he and I may consult off the record. Basically, he's an observer. Will that be satisfactory?" Newton asked.

Kline motioned to Jones.

"I think we'd better discuss this."

They went down the hall to ensure privacy.

"Jefferson, what do you think about House sitting in on the depositions? And should we include the university in this suit? We haven't even talked about that before."

"We could include them," Jones answered, "but it would

delay things by several weeks, at best, and probably several months. We would have to refile all the papers, and they would certainly demand time to prepare, even though I'm certain they've known about this all along. Then we'd have to depose each of their faculty members who've been involved, both maternal-fetal and neonatal. The university isn't known for being speedy, and the Smiths want a rapid conclusion."

"I know." Kline looked downcast. "I didn't include them because I felt that all the blame rested on Dr. Jankowski. Plus, we have plenty of support from Thomas and Segal. It doesn't matter anyway. The university maternal-fetal people are secondary, casual consultants. They didn't actually see or examine Angie. None of the decisions were made by them."

"You're right, of course," Jones nodded. "It would make things more difficult, trying to explain their role to a jury, and it would definitely delay this process by quite a bit. I think negotiating a settlement would also be more difficult with three parties on the other side. The university has never settled anything, as far as I know."

"How about House? Should we let him sit in?" Kline queried.

"I can't see any harm in it, so I suppose it's okay," Jones answered, reluctantly.

"Let's go, then."

They went back to Thomas's office.

"It's okay with us that Mr. House is an observer," Kline directed his answer to Newton, "but we do reserve the right to object if his participation turns out to be something more. Do you concur, Dr. Thomas?"

"Yes," Thomas answered grudgingly.

"That settled then, this deposition is in reference to the Smith baby. I assume you know how depositions work. Any questions before we begin?" Kline asked.

"I don't have any questions," Thomas bristled.

"Then let's begin."

"Do you swear to tell the truth, the whole truth, and nothing but the truth?" the court reporter asked.

"I do."

"Please state your full name," Newton began.

"Dr. George Thomas."

"What is your country of origin?"

"New Zealand."

"Are you now a permanent resident of the United States?"

"Yes."

"Are you a resident of this city?"

"Yes.

"How long have you lived here?"

"Eight years, since I joined the faculty at the medical school."

Newton and House shared a legal pad covered with lists of questions. House took notes as Newton worked his way through the pages. Occasionally, he wrote a note to Newton.

"Are you a physician?"

"Yes, I am."

"Where did you obtain your medical education?"

"I graduated from medical school in New Zealand and completed a residency in pediatrics there. I came to the United States for a fellowship in neonatology, which I completed at UCLA."

"I assume that means the University of California at Los Angeles?"

"Yes, of course."

"Did you come here from your fellowship at UCLA?"

"No. I stayed on the faculty there for five years before coming here."

"You seem a bit older than that. I can't account for the years."

"I was in practice in New Zealand for eight years before I came to this country."

"Thank you. Are you board certified?"

"Yes, in both pediatrics and neonatology."

"Are you licensed to practice medicine in Missouri?"

"Yes, I am."

"Are you a member of the faculty of the Missouri State Medical School?"

"Yes. I'm an associate professor with tenure." Thomas's answers were clipped and cold. He sat straight up in his chair, with his hands folded on his desk and his feet planted squarely on the floor. He held his head high, chin up, as if daring Newton to come after him.

"How long have you been an associate professor?"

Kline interrupted.

"Dr. Thomas's curriculum vitae and bibliography are presented to be attached to the record, and we will stipulate to the facts contained therein."

"Are you head of neonatology?" Newton continued.

"No, I'm not."

"Isn't it true that a more junior person was appointed over you?"

"Yes, but I wasn't really interested in the position."

"Are you familiar with the Smith baby, William N. Smith, Jr.?"

"Yes. I took over his care the morning after he was delivered, and I am currently his principal physician."

"Please describe your findings when you first saw him."

"It was shortly after his birth, about thirty minutes, when one of the university neonatologists first saw him. He was reported by the Memorial neonatologist to be limp and floppy at birth with a faint shrill cry. The Apgar scores were two and four."

"I'm afraid I must interrupt. Please explain what Apgar means."

"Virginia Apgar was a physician who devised a ten-point score for assessing newborns based on heart rate, breathing, color, muscle tone, and reflex irritability. It's done at one and five minutes after birth.

"Are these scores low or high?"

"They are low and ominous, especially the five-minute score of four."

"Please continue."

"Otherwise he seemed normal. Those findings remained when I first saw him early the next morning. He has not improved since then. In fact, his condition has worsened in that he has developed the spasticity typical of cerebral palsy. He does not suck and rarely swallows, requiring all feedings be given through a tube down his nose, throat, and esophagus to his stomach. He requires constant attention and care, and he is expected to be profoundly retarded. In short, this baby has classic, profound CP plus severe mental retardation with no hope of ever being normal."

"Do you have a professional opinion as to the cause of the cerebral palsy?"

"I think that the brain damage resulting in this baby's CP was directly caused by the failure of Dr. Janet Jankowski to respond in a timely fashion to the initial severe drop in the baby's heart rate during labor."

"Are you saying that this baby would be normal if she had responded more quickly?"

"Absolutely."

"Since you knew the baby was having some difficulties, and since you had an opinion as to the source of these problems, why did you fail to report the situation to the risk management committee at Memorial Hospital?"

"It didn't occur to me. If it had, I would have assumed that

Dr. Jankowski had that duty."

"Haven't you received our instruction manual indicating the requirement that you report any incident that might result in legal action?"

"No. Remember, I'm a consultant at Memorial. My liability insurance is through the university, not you."

"Doesn't the university have the same requirement?"

"Objection," Kline interrupted. "It's not relevant."

"Withdrawn. Isn't it true that neonatology is the science and discipline of the care of the newborn, not of pregnant women? Isn't the care of the pregnant woman the province of the obstetrician and the maternal-fetal medicine specialist?"

"That's two questions," Kline observed.

"Okay, please answer the first one," Newton instructed Thomas.

"What was the first question again?" he asked. Thomas smiled smugly.

"Isn't it true," the court reporter replied, "that neonatology is the science and discipline of the care of the newborn, not of pregnant women?"

"Yes. Now what was the second one?" Thomas answered curtly.

The court reporter again replied.

"Isn't the care of the pregnant woman the province of the obstetrician and the maternal-fetal medicine specialist?"

"That is true, but anyone with any experience in neonatology spends enough time in the labor suite and delivery room working with the obstetrician and maternal-fetal specialist to become expert in recognizing delays or failures to act. It is my professional opinion that prompt delivery of this baby by cesarean section immediately after the first drop in heart rate would have resulted in a normal newborn."

Newton's exasperation was apparent in his voice.

"Let me summarize. You're stating that all the damage occurred with the second drop in heart rate and that a cesarean section before the second drop would have prevented any damage to this baby."

"That's correct."

"You do know that Dr. Jankowski did consult with the maternal-fetal medicine specialists at that time and that they agreed with her care?"

"I understand. They were just trying to protect her."

"Protect her from what? Their consultation was before the second dip."

"She didn't want to do a c-section then, and they went along with her."

"Are you accusing the recognized specialists in this field of a cover-up?"

"I didn't say it that way. Unless the consultants vigorously disagree, their tendency is to be supportive. Dr. Jankowski chose not to act, since the heart rate did return to normal, and the maternal-fetal medicine specialists went along with her. I think they were mistaken. Please note that the second drop in heart rate was deep and prolonged. Had it not occurred, my opinion is that this baby would be normal."

"If you will look at the fetal monitor tracing, which displays the baby's heart rate from the time Mrs. Smith entered the labor suite, you must see that there is very little to no beat-to-beat variability." Newton handed him the tracing.

Thomas spent a few minutes flipping through the tracing.

"Yes. I see it now, and I saw it after the delivery when I looked at the records before I first examined the baby."

"Isn't the lack of beat-to-beat variability considered a warning sign that something is wrong? And isn't it true that the timing in this case would indicate that whatever was wrong preceded labor?"

"That's two questions again," Kline interrupted.

118

However, Thomas answered before Kline finished.

"That could be true, but I definitely don't think so here. However, beat-to-beat variability or the lack of it is relatively non-specific and has many causes. The most common one is perfectly normal, and it occurs when the baby sleeps. Babies sleep for periods of thirty to forty-five minutes fairly frequently throughout the day and night, unless they are stimulated."

"Wouldn't you consider labor to be stimulating?"

"Yes, of course I would. However, Mrs. Smith was in very early labor when she came in, and she asked to have an epidural anesthesia catheter inserted soon after she got there, before her labor had a chance to become much of a stimulus to the baby. Loss of beat-to-beat variability with epidural anesthesia is not uncommon. I think that explains the occurrence and answers your questions."

"This is your professional opinion, even though you're not an expert in the field?"

"Yes, it is. I certainly have enough experience to recognize incompetence when I see it."

"Did you communicate your opinion about Dr. Jankowski's care to Mrs. Smith?"

"Yes, to both Mr. and Mrs. Smith on the morning after the cesarean section when I first saw her and when she was fully awake from her general anesthesia so she could comprehend the rather major problems I was describing to her."

"Did you see her at other times?"

"Yes, I did."

"When, if you don't mind?"

"Twice a day for as long as she was there."

"Did you discuss the baby with her each time?"

"Of course, with both of them."

"Did you tell her each time that you thought Dr. Jankowski was in error?"

"Yes, I'm sure I did, if the subject came up."

"Did it?"

"Yes."

"Did you also write these opinions for the record?"

"Yes, I did, in both the mother's and baby's charts. I felt then and still feel that it was my professional duty to do so."

"Again, you do recognize that the maternal-fetal medicine specialists had already written a contrary opinion in the mother's record, dated and timed just after the end of the first dip."

"Yes, I saw it when I made my own entry. I disagree with them."

"Isn't it a general rule that physicians prefer to discuss differing opinions in person before writing them down for the record?"

"I suppose so. However, in this case, I feel now, and felt then, that the quality of care given by Dr. Jankowski was compromised sufficiently that it was my ethical and moral obligation to enter my opinion for the record."

House asked Newton to go off the record, and the two went to whisper in the corner of the room. The others stood up to stretch.

"Clark, I'm sure you're going to ask anyway, but I really would like to get a feel for how much legal work this guy does."

"I agree, Chester. In fact, I think that right now is a good time to get into that problem. If you have suggestions, interrupt me at anytime. We're both going to have to tighten our procedures for reporting incidents, whether it's for the regular staff or for consultants."

"I agree. Let's see how this goes."

Newton called the deposition to order.

"How many professional liability cases do you become involved with each year?"

"I think I've reviewed eighteen or twenty over the last year. It's been that many every year for several years now."

"For exactly how many years have you been doing this?"

"For the past five or six."

"How many of those have been for the plaintiff?"

"Most of them are."

"Since you are now the neonatology expert witness for the plaintiff in this case, doesn't it seem to be a conflict of interest for you to write a differing opinion in the record? In fact, that opinion is the entire basis for this proceeding."

"I resent your implication."

"Your resentment is noted. The facts speak for themselves. First, your opinion does differ from that of the recognized specialists in the area. Second, you entered that differing opinion in the record. Third, a lawsuit has been filed. Fourth, you are an expert for the plaintiff. Fifth, much or most of the case rests on your opinion. Finally, you failed to notify the risk management committee at Memorial Hospital of the event. That, to me, represents some conflict of interest."

"I believe you will find that others agree with me. I am just doing my duty as a responsible physician."

"Ask him if he has ever done any defense work," House whispered. "I'll bet he hasn't."

"Have you ever testified, given a deposition, or reviewed records for the defendant?" Newton asked.

"I'm certain I have," Thomas answered.

"Would you name the case for me, please?"

"I don't have it on the tip of my tongue. It was several years ago."

"You mean that you remember the eighteen or twenty cases a year for the past five or six years for the plaintiff, but you cannot remember the one case you did for a defendant. Isn't it true that you have the reputation of being a plaintiff's expert and that you enjoy a large income from that enterprise? Don't answer. Those are all the questions I have."

Kline then spoke.

"Would you please restate your professional opinion in reference to this case?"

"It is my professional opinion that the brain damage resulting in cerebral palsy and almost certain profound mental retardation for William N. Smith, Jr. was caused by Dr. Janet Jankowski's delay in reacting to the first drop in heart rate and that if she had reacted promptly by doing a cesarean section immediately, this baby would be entirely normal."

There were no further questions.

"I think Thomas did a good job for us, don't you?" Kline asked Jones when they were back in their office. "The conflict of interest thing is not important, assuming Thomas is correct. That sort of thing happens all the time with medical experts from major referral centers. If necessary, I suppose we could use him as a witness of fact and find another expert in neonatology. But I'd rather keep him where he is. He'll behave better if we're paying him."

"Yeah, he did a good job, but he sure is arrogant. I hope that won't hurt us. Segal, the maternal-fetal expert, is more important, though, and perhaps more overbearing," Jones said. "Our whole case hinges on him." He paused. "Herb, I'm still bothered by the lack of beat-to-beat variability. There's something about this case that just nags at me. Something isn't quite right."

Kline paused.

"I feel okay about it so far. Let's see how things go."

"Is Segal next?"

"Yes, next week."

"Herb, I'm surprised Newton hasn't let us depose Dr. Jankowski yet. We've always done the adversaries as the first depositions in all our previous cases."

"That's true," Kline answered slowly. "I suppose he's trying to let her learn from reading Thomas's and Segal's depositions. Any-

122

how, they were immediately available, and I wanted to come out swinging. The Smiths want to go as fast as possible, so I agreed. I don't think it will make a difference."

"I expect you're right," Jones answered. He left Kline's office and went into his own.

Newton met with his risk-management committee to summarize the deposition.

"Thomas is adamant that delay caused the damage. I don't think we'll shake him on that, so we'll just have to prove him wrong. The only thing that might help, so far, is that he's done eighteen to twenty plaintiff cases per year for the past several years. He's had only one defense case, which he can't remember, if it ever occurred. We'll have to keep that record in mind when this case is over. I'm sure the dean will be interested. Segal will probably be just as bad when we get to him. Do we have anything new that might help?" Newton asked.

"Nothing yet. The baby is the same. There's been no improvement for weeks now. The CMV was negative. The CT scan is scheduled in a week or so, but it's unlikely that it'll help. They usually don't in this type of case," the pediatric member answered.

"I talked with the anesthesiologist who took care of Mrs. Smith," Newton said. "He agrees with everyone else that there were no problems with either the epidural or the general anesthetic she received. So, that's not an issue, at least so far. It's curious Kline didn't include the anesthesiologists. Usually they are prime targets for the plaintiff. I hope it's more overconfidence."

They went through the case again, in detail, as they did each week, just to be sure nothing had been missed. Then Newton asked Janet for comments, but she didn't answer.

"The deposition for Segal is next week," Newton said. "I'll report back to you after that."

House met with his committee, also, and he reported much the same to them. They were quite upset with the number of cases Thomas participated in annually. The problem of the cases being all for the plaintiff was duly noted.

"Mike, I've reached my limit," Janet pounced on him as soon as he walked through the door at home. "It's almost like that jerk Thomas is trying to run me out of practice. He really went after my quality of care in his deposition, from what Clark told us at the committee meeting. I know he's wrong, but it's tough not being affected by some of it. I think the committee supports me, but I'm very angry."

"I'm sorry, honey. How are things otherwise?"

"My biggest problem is the amount of time I have to spend on this case. It's affecting my practice. I'm seeing fewer patients, either new or old, and I'm not worth much around here either. On top of that, I've missed a bunch of deliveries just being at the committee meetings or preparing for them. Patients don't expect that, and I lose the income."

She sat morosely at the dinner table that evening, her plate a mess from pushing her food around. The children had finished quickly and were watching TV. Finally, she took her plate to the sink and retreated to the study to resume staring blankly at her lap.

The telephone snapped Janet awake; one of her patients was in labor.

15

"Angie, how's work going?" Bill bent over the arm of the chair to hug her after he walked through the door and into the family room.

"Bill, I never see you there. I was beginning to wonder if you had forgotten that I was back at work. You're gone from the office all the time, visiting clients or taking them to lunch. When you are there, why don't you stop by to see how I'm doing?"

"Honey, that's not fair." Bill backed away. "You know I have to spend some time each month or so with each of our major accounts, usually in their offices. I'm still meeting some of their people for the first time. Being the sales manager is taking a lot more time than I ever imagined. I'll be sure to stop by tomorrow. Anyway, when are you going to be promoted?"

"They're waiting a little while to let me get used to being back at work, and I think they want me full-time before I get the promotion, so I don't know. Soon I hope." She almost smiled.

"Is anything new with the baby?"

"His name is Will, or have you forgotten?" she shot back. "Nothing is new. I think they'll put that tube in his stomach this week, so he can be fed more easily and safely. Then I'm sure they'll want to send him home. Wilma can take care of him."

"What do they say about his chances for . . . "

"Nothing at all," she said with finality. "The last I heard was a week ago, when the resident said there was almost no chance he would do anything but grow, and not very well at that. They call it vegetating, which really sounds horrible. So there's no chance for improvement."

"That's pretty much what they told me two days ago when I went by," Bill groused. "Honey, I do remember that his name is Will. It's just hard to put a name on something that isn't normal and never will be. He should be smiling by now, according to the baby books, and following us with his eyes. He doesn't do either one."

"I know that, Bill. I've been there several times this week also. I know all about it."

"I'm sorry, Angie."

More than four months after the delivery, Angie and Bill still had not resumed making love, which was upsetting to both of them. Angie couldn't understand why she had no desire at all. She remembered all the good times before her pregnancy and delivery, and she was baffled by her lack of response. Nothing seemed to work. She brooded about it, staring into space and feeling empty. She knew Bill was frustrated, but she couldn't help it.

Because of their obvious distress over the baby and the disruption of ordinary family activity, he finally suggested getting help.

"Angie, we don't seem to get any better," he said timidly later that evening. "Neither of us, and especially you, has bounced back since the delivery. Physically, we should be fine, and you're not. And I'm worried about our mental status. I think we both need help. Please come see a counselor with me."

"Bill, the thing that would help the most is to get this lawsuit over with."

"That will help, I agree, but winning the lawsuit isn't enough. We need to get the rest of our life back to normal. Please think about it," Bill begged her.

"Not now. Maybe when it's over. Right now I want to concentrate on the lawsuit and on work," she announced firmly.

"Okay," was Bill's only response. In spite of her objections, he began to search for a counselor.

"Dr. Johnson, Dr. Jankowski, your wife's father, is on the phone."

"Good afternoon, Mike. Sorry to call you at the office, but Margaret and I wanted to talk to you about Janet. Have you got a few minutes?" It was just before five o'clock.

"Jim, I'm just about to see my last patient. Can I call you back when I'm finished?"

"Sure. We're at home."

"It'll be thirty minutes or so."

He returned the call forty minutes later.

"Hi, it's Mike."

"Thanks for calling back. Mike, you know we've usually talked to Janet once a week. She and Margaret used to spend hours on the phone together. Since the delivery of that baby with CP, it's been more often, until the last two or three weeks. Now she doesn't seem to want to call or talk at all. And when we do talk, it's always very brief. We're getting worried because of the way she sounds and because she doesn't want to talk. Is she all right?"

"I think so, Jim. Truthfully, she doesn't say very much to me either, and when she does, it's the same thing over and over. This whole thing has really thrown her for a loop, but I think she's holding up okay." Mike talked in circles.

Jim was more direct. "Mike, I think she's seriously depressed, and we want to help."

"I guess you're right, Jim. I haven't talked to anyone about it yet, so I haven't had a reason to verbalize my fears," Mike admitted.

"Mike, are you two okay?" Margaret interrupted, on another telephone.

"Yes, I think we are. We're spending a lot of time together because Janet hasn't wanted to do much except go to dinner or the movies occasionally. She hasn't wanted to do anything social otherwise since the newspaper article. Actually, I think we're closer than we've ever been," Mike responded slowly, clearly weighing each word.

"Well, I'm glad to hear that," Margaret answered.

"Jim, Margaret, what I don't know is where this will end. These darn lawsuits are so hard to predict, as you know. The depositions seem to be going about as expected." He summarized them. "I know she didn't do anything wrong, but that doesn't mean she'll win. Whatever the result, I don't think I can predict what she'll do afterwards. Her practice is taking a beating because of all the time she needs for reading and meetings. I'll try to be more on top of her mood. It may be that she needs to see someone," he thought out loud.

"How are Carol and Michael doing?" Margaret asked.

"They're okay, but there's no question that they know their mother's upset. I try to tell them that it's because she's working too hard and that it'll get better. I'm not sure they believe me. They even asked me if we were getting divorced. I guess that's a sign of the times. Janet's been trying to spend more time with them, which has helped some. I think they'll be fine. We've been careful to make sure that they know we love them and each other."

"I'm sure they'll be okay. Mike, we'll call you once in a while, and you can call us anytime, especially if we can help. Okay?" Jim asked.

"I will. I'm glad you called. I should have called you before this, but I get too wrapped up in work and Janet, and then I forget," Mike confessed. "I'll try to call each week."

16

Segal had also insisted on his own office for his deposition. It was large, elegant, and extremely neat. The walls, tables, and shelves were covered with certificates, diplomas, and awards, which Newton had a chance to examine carefully; Segal kept them waiting thirty minutes while he consulted on a possible cesarean section. Newton did not recognize many of the organizations or places represented on these documents. *Interesting,* he thought.

Segal finally came bustling in. During the introductions, he formally shook hands with each of them, rearranged the seating, and picked at microscopic lint on his trousers and desk. After all the fuss and show, he said he was ready.

"Dr. Segal, this is Clark Newton, who is the attorney for Dr. Jankowski and Memorial Hospital. I think you know my partner, Jefferson Jones. I know you've been given depositions before, but do you have any questions before we start?" asked Kline.

"No, I don't think so."

"Then, let's go."

"Do you swear to tell the truth, the whole truth, and nothing but the truth?" asked the court reporter.

"I do."

"Please state your full name." Newton began with his customary request.

"Joseph Segal, M.D."

"Are you a resident of this city?"

"Yes."

"Where are you from?"

"I was born and raised in New York City."

"Where did you obtain your medical education?"

"In the northeast. I graduated from Mt. Sinai Medical School and completed a residency in obstetrics and gynecology in Boston." Segal appeared at his "English" best; he was wearing a three-piece European-cut suit and tie, a white shirt, and Italian shoes. His accent was carefully cultured, and his demeanor was arrogant.

"Are you subspecialty trained?"

"Yes. Following residency, I completed a two-year fellowship in maternal-fetal medicine in Philadelphia."

"Are you board certified?"

"Yes, in both obstetrics and gynecology and maternal-fetal medicine by the American Board of Obstetrics and Gynecology."

"Did you move here after your fellowship?"

"No. I obtained a position on the staff of a teaching hospital in New Jersey."

"Why did you move here?"

"I was offered the chance to be head of maternal-fetal medicine at Cloud View Hospital."

"Is that where you are currently practicing?"

"Yes. I have been head of maternal-fetal medicine here at Cloud View Hospital for the past seven years."

"Are you licensed in Missouri?"

"Yes."

Kline spoke up.

"Dr. Segal's curriculum vitae and bibliography are entered into the record."

"Thank you," Newton said. He worked from a legal pad, but he wrote in some of the questions as he thought of them. "Is Cloud View a teaching hospital?"

"No. It's a community hospital."

"Isn't it unusual to leave a teaching hospital for a community hospital?"

"No. The need for service is just as great, and Cloud View put together a nice package to get me here."

"How many people do you have in your division or section?"

"All the obstetricians on the staff here at the hospital."

"What I was asking is, are there any other full-time people with you?"

"No. Only in other departments."

"Are there any other maternal-fetal medicine specialists at Cloud View?"

"No."

"Why is that?"

"We've never seen the need for more."

"Are you paid for consultations such as the one you just did before the deposition?"

"Yes."

"Objection. I can't see where this is leading," interrupted Kline.

"That's all I have on that score," Newton reassured him. "Dr. Segal, I can't help noticing the plaques and certificates you have displayed in your office. I see they are listed in your curriculum vitae. Please tell me what they're for."

"These over here are certificates and diplomas attesting to my training and recognition as a maternal-fetal medicine specialist."

"What are the others?"

"Most of them are honorary memberships in obstetrical and gynecological societies in cities where I have been a visiting speaker."

"I looked, but I don't see the New York Obstetrical Society, the Chicago Gynecological Society, or even the St. Louis Society. I believe they are three of the most prestigious in the United States."

"No, they aren't there." Segal quickly glared at Newton.

"Are you a member of the St. Louis Gynecological Society?"

"No. I haven't been asked to join."

"If I'm correct, all of these certificates are from relatively small towns rather than from major cities. Is that correct?"

"Yes, but I think those communities deserve the chance for continuing medical education as well, don't you?"

"Of course. What is your topic when you speak to these groups?"

"How the practitioner can cut his or her risk of being sued."

"Do you consider yourself to be an expert on this subject?"

"I think so. There doesn't seem to be any decrease in demand for me to speak." Segal remained cool and calm, the picture of control.

"How many such visits do you make a year?"

"I usually do two or three a month."

"Are you paid for these talks?"

"Yes."

"Do you attend professional society meetings also?"

"Yes."

"How many per year?"

"There are four or five I think are important. I usually attend each of them."

"Do you speak at those also?"

"No, I haven't so far."

"If I may summarize, you speak two or three times a month on professional liability in small communities all over the country. Each must involve at least two days to allow travel to out-of-the-way places. In addition, you attend a major meeting every other month, which must take another four or five days. That comes to at least three working weeks out of every eight away from home. Is that correct?"

"Yes, I guess so."

"Dr. Segal, are you familiar with the Smith case?"

"Yes, I am."

"Would you give us your opinion concerning the care of Mrs. Smith during her pregnancy by Dr. Jankowski?"

"Yes. I think it was abominable."

Newton's dislike for Segal became intense, and he found it difficult to be civil to him. He increasingly felt that Kline would do anything and use anybody to win a case.

"That's hardly a medical term. Can you be more specific?"

"Dr. Jankowski failed to react to the first drop in heart rate as shown here on the fetal monitor tracing."

"Are you saying that she didn't react at all?"

"Yes."

"What about the oxygen, the position change, and the increased IV fluids?"

"That was just gilding the lily."

"I don't believe that's exactly medical terminology either."

"Pardon me. Those three actions have been the rule since the beginning of monitoring. I don't believe they do any good, especially in this baby's case. The only thing which would have worked is a cesarean section. Just as important is the fact that it took seventeen minutes to get the baby delivered when the second drop occurred. Had she reacted promptly to the first drop, this baby would have been normal."

"Are you saying that seventeen minutes isn't fast enough to move to the operating room, perform a cesarean section, and actually deliver the baby? The guidelines of the American College of Obstetricians and Gynecologists indicate that thirty minutes from making the decision to starting the section, not delivery, is the national standard."

"Yes, I am stating that it isn't fast enough. They had more than enough warning thirty minutes earlier with the first drop in heart rate. I might accept thirty minutes earlier with the first drop in heart rate. I might accept seventeen minutes if Dr. Jankowski had responded appropriately with the first episode."

"What is the standard at this hospital where you are the chief?"

"Fifteen minutes."

"To starting the section or to delivery?"

"To delivery. I thought I made that clear."

"What is the cesarean section rate at your hospital?"

"Objection. I don't think that's relevant," Kline broke in.

"We'll disagree in front of the judge. Please ask your expert to answer the question." Newton stood firm on the issue.

"Answer the question, Dr. Segal," Kline instructed him.

"Our cesarean section rate is thirty-five percent."

"Is that the total cesarean section rate or the primary rate?"

"The total rate."

"Isn't it true that the national rate is about twenty-three percent and that the American College of Obstetricians and Gynecologists is continually looking at ways to lower it to near twenty percent, or even less?"

"I object for the record, again. You may answer, Dr. Segal," said Kline.

"I suppose so."

"Please answer with either a yes or a no," demanded Newton.

"Yes."

"It would seem that the rate at Cloud View, where you are in charge, is much higher than the national standard. How do you explain that?"

"We feel we provide excellent care and that our mortality and morbidity statistics are equal to any institution in the area."

"But not better, isn't that correct?"

"Yes."

"It seems to me that you advocate a very liberal cesarean section policy with no benefit for the patient or her baby. Do you charge more for cesarean section?"

"Objection."

"Withdrawn. Isn't it true that the complication rate and the mortality rate for a woman undergoing a cesarean section are several times higher than for those women who have vaginal deliveries?"

"Yes."

"As I understand it, you advocate and accept a cesarean section rate at Cloud View that is much higher than the national standard, with no improvement in outcome. In addition, the risk for the mother is significantly higher when a cesarean section is performed. How does that qualify you to be an expert in this case, to be able to give us an objective professional opinion?"

"I have been educated through medical school and residency and certified by the American Board of Obstetrics and Gynecology. In addition, I am fully trained and certified in maternal-fetal medicine by the same board. I was a respected faculty member for five years before coming here. I have been the chief of maternal-fetal medicine at Cloud View Hospital, a major institution in this city, for seven years, with a successful record. The issue is moot, it seems to me."

"You indicated earlier that you had reviewed the fetal monitor tracing. Did you notice the lack of beat-to-beat variability from the time Mrs. Smith came in?"

"Yes."

"In your opinion, what is the cause of that, and what is its significance?"

"That's two questions," observed Kline.

"Sorry. What is the cause of the lack of beat-to-beat variability?"

"I can't be certain, but it is my impression that it was a normal occurrence, most likely due to the baby being in a sleep cycle, and then to the epidural anesthesia which was given quite early in her labor."

"Does that mean that you attach no significance to the lack of beat-to-beat variability?"

"No, I don't think so."

"Please be specific."

"I attach no significance to the lack of beat-to-beat variability. I explain it as I have already indicated."

"Why is it that you are so uncertain?"

"Medicine is an art, not a science. It's frequently impossible to be certain."

"Obviously, that reasoning applies to cesarean sections as well. You said the epidural might cause the lack of variability. Have you examined the anesthesia records in this case?"

"Yes, of course."

"Are you qualified to have an opinion about the anesthesia as a cause of this baby's problems?"

"As you know, I am not an anesthesiologist, and I am not certified as such. However, I have spent enough time working with our anesthesiologists here and elsewhere to have an opinion."

"Will you share that opinion with us?"

"Of course. Anesthesia was not a factor in the difficulties this baby had. The fault is entirely Dr. Jankowski's."

"How many professional liability cases do you review annually?"

"Twenty to thirty."

Newton was incredulous.

"Twenty to thirty. These cases, plus all the time you spend speaking about liability or attending meetings leave you very little time to work at the hospital. How do you have time to do anything else?"

"I work very hard."

"How many of those cases are for the plaintiff?"

"Most of them."

"Can you tell me the last case you reviewed for the defense?"

"Yes, we had one against us two years ago."

"Have there been others for the defense?"

"None I can recall."

"In other words, your involvement in professional liability cases is limited to being an expert for the plaintiff, except for the one case in which you and your institution were the defendants. How many years have you been an expert for the plaintiff?"

"Since I came to Cloud View, seven years ago. I did only a few prior to that."

"I must question whether there is some conflict of interest here. You are a plaintiff's expert, by your own testimony. You do twenty to thirty cases per year. You must be earning a very large income from this activity. The need to perpetuate this activity may color your thinking. This is especially so, given the high cesarean section rate at your hospital."

Kline stood up.

"Objection."

"That's all I have," Newton said.

Kline remained standing.

"Dr. Segal, would you please state your professional opinion again concerning this case?"

"It is my professional opinion that Dr. Janet Jankowski's failure to respond to the first drop in the fetal heart rate with an immediate cesarean section is the cause of the cerebral palsy and certain mental retardation in this baby. If she had responded in a timely manner, this baby would have been normal."

"Nothing further," said Kline. He sat down.

"Nothing further from me, either. I think that's all," said Jones.

"I agree." Newton got up to leave.

"Herb, this deposition didn't go as well as Thomas's did. I'm a little unhappy about where we are. Segal is just too slick, and he clearly spends too much time as a plaintiff witness and liability speaker to be able to do anything else. On top of that, he must have a huge income from the hospital, plus all the consulting for cesarean sections. I'll bet they even call him when he's out of town. He won't look good to a jury. Newton will hit hard on all of these points." They were sitting in Jones's office.

"I agree. Also, I'm really worried about the cesarean section rate at his hospital. Thank God, we aren't being retained by them. They might be difficult to defend. At any rate, I think our case is solid enough that we'll be okay. I'll try to coach him, as much as he will allow me to, on how to behave with a judge and jury," Kline answered, but with a worried look on his face.

"I'm also upset by his almost cavalier way of ignoring the lack of beat-to-beat variability. I think Clark will hit on that hard. Have we got anything else pending?" Jones asked.

"Everything else is on hold, so we can spend all our time on this one. Actually, there isn't that much anyway. We depose Dr. Jankowski next, so we need to be ready."

"Okay. See you later," Jones called to Kline as he left for lunch.

Newton described the deposition to House and then discussed it with his risk-management committee.

"This guy, Segal, is even more of a hired gun than Thomas. He must spend full time working on liability cases, if the number he claims he is doing is correct. In addition, he travels all the time to small hospitals talking about liability prevention. He attends several national meetings a year, but he is never asked to participate. And he hasn't been asked to join the St. Louis Gynecological Society. Both Janet and Kim are members. Interesting."

Newton shuffled his papers and continued.

"He was firm on the issue of there being a delay in performing the cesarean section, but he was wishy-washy about the lack of beat-to-beat variability. Curiously, the cesarean section rate at Cloud View, his hospital, is thirty-five percent. Not surprisingly, he seems to consult on most of those cesareans, and he is paid a separate fee for it. We'll be able to use that against him. Let's make sure that you, Janet, and Kim Workman are prepared to answer questions about cesarean section rates and about the beat-to-beat variability."

Janet nodded agreement.

"I guess that's all," Newton said. He started to stand. "Oh, yes. I should have taken care of this sooner. We need to find a neonatologist who can review the records and be our expert. I had hoped we could use someone in the department here or at the university, but that's out now because of Thomas. Any suggestions?"

"How about Alex Dobbins at Seacroft Hospital? He's in charge of the NICU there. He's very good, and he should make a good witness. I don't know what his schedule is, but he's worth a try," the pediatrician member suggested.

"Sounds good to me. I'll give him a call. I guess that's all for today." Newton promptly went to his telephone.

"Dr. Dobbins, this is Clark Newton. I'm the attorney for Memorial Hospital. I hope this isn't a bad time?" He was pleased to get through so quickly.

"No. What's the problem?"

"Isn't that always the way?" Newton joked. "I never meet or talk to anyone new without there being a problem. I'd like to meet with you and show you a set of labor and delivery and newborn records, hoping you will agree to be an expert for us, defending the hospital and the obstetrician, Dr. Janet Jankowski. Can you do it, and when can we meet?" Newton spent a little time explaining the case.

"Yes, I can," Dobbins answered. "How about early next week? If you can have the records and depositions, so far, delivered to me today, I'll look at them over the weekend, so I'm prepared. Since I don't know anything about the case, other than what you just told me, you must realize that I may feel I can't help, that you should settle. Can you come here?"

"I understand you first need to see the records to make a decision. In fact, I'd be bothered if you didn't feel that way," Newton answered. "I'll send everything to you immediately, and your office is fine. And please, we want you to be objective and critical. How's two o'clock on Monday?"

"Fine. See you then."

Janet and Mike decided to go out to dinner at Garibaldi's. Once seated, they ordered their favorite fish and white wine.

"So, what happened today? It has to have something to do with the case," Mike asked as they were drinking their wine before the swordfish arrived.

"It does, as always. The experts for the Smiths are at me again. The maternal-fetal guy, Segal, was especially bad from what Newton told us. He thinks he can counter Segal with our own experts, but it still hurts to hear all the things Segal said. Newton assures me that the risk-management committee is unswayed in their support for me. I guess that makes me feel better."

Janet ate very little and just pushed her fish around her plate. She gulped two glasses of wine and started on a third. She was preoccupied with her thoughts about the suit, and then she became a little sleepy. Mike finally took her home.

When they got there, Janet rushed to the toilet, where she promptly threw up what little she had eaten. She was tipsy from the wine, but she felt a little better once she freshened up. She and Mike tried to talk, but she fell asleep again, so Mike led her to bed.

17

"Hi, I'm Clark Newton."

"Alex Dobbins." Dobbins was a tall, slender, stooped man, who wore bow ties and short-sleeved shirts. His white coat hung on the back of the door, and his office was cluttered with medical journals, books, and reprints of articles, all in some order, which Newton doubted was helpful. Dobbins seemed charming and genuine, and he seemed to want to help.

"Did you get a chance to look at the records?"

"Yes. This is really a difficult case, especially with the feeding tube through the baby's belly. It will look terrible to both judge and jury, but maybe I can help."

They talked for an hour about the details of the case.

"Who are the plaintiff experts?" Dobbins asked.

"Dr. George Thomas is the neonatologist, as you know from his deposition, and Dr. Joseph Segal is the maternal-fetal expert. Here's a copy of his deposition, which I just received." Newton handed him the sheaf of paper.

"Thanks. I might have known. It figured when you had to go outside the university pediatrics department to use me. Those two guys seem to do nothing else but work for the plaintiff. Kline and Jones are pretty successful at being plaintiff advocates. From what I hear, it's unusual for them to take a case as a gamble, so that makes this one even harder to defend."

"Unfortunately, you're right," Newton answered.

"I must say, I am confused about why they didn't name the university maternal-fetal consultants in the suit. They were very much involved, and the university is another very deep pocket. My guess is that they were afraid that there would be too much pressure on Thomas, but I think that's unlikely. He'll do or say anything. Maybe they're afraid of the university. This seems to be a big mistake on their part." Dobbins paused to collect his thoughts.

Newton nodded and stretched.

"I'm sure their position will be that Dr. Jankowski should have responded earlier to the drop in the fetal heart rate with an emergency cesarean section right then, before the second drop ever happened."

"That's what both Segal and Thomas said," Newton answered.

"I think Janet Jankowski did everything correctly. I can't find any error on her part. Something happened to this baby before labor ever started. Our problem will be to prove I'm right." Dobbins stretched while he deliberated. "The fact that all current theory and opinion supports me about cerebral palsy may not make much difference with either a judge or jury. They look at the bad baby and the distraught family first."

"This is the first real encouragement I've had in this case," Newton said, smiling.

"Dr. Jankowski even did a culture for group B streptococcus, which was negative. That's good thinking on her part and, fortunately, this baby had no evidence of infection, and Mrs. Smith's temperature was never above ninety-nine-point-six degrees during her entire stay in the hospital."

"Kim Workman is our maternal-fetal expert, and she agrees with you, but she doesn't say it quite as eloquently," Newton responded. "We still have to overcome the two drops in heart rate, and some rather slick testimony by Thomas and Segal. How about the baby right now?"

"This baby is really bad. I agree he will be profoundly

retarded. Doing a gastrostomy and placing a feeding tube through it will facilitate sending him home, but he will have to have almost constant care. If he never learns to suck and swallow, and I'm sure he won't from what I read in the chart, it's my guess that his life expectancy will be very brief, one or two years at the most. Sooner or later, he'll have some of the feeding go back up his esophagus, and he'll be unable to handle it, and he'll choke. Some of it will go down into his lungs, and he'll get pneumonia. A couple of episodes of lung infection will be all it takes to cause him to die, no matter what's done about it."

"Isn't there any way to prevent this happening?" Newton asked.

Dobbins shook his head.

"I notice Thomas agreed to a CT scan," he continued. "I'm surprised. It's unlikely it will show much, but he usually won't agree to anything that might jeopardize his case and fee. I'd like to know the results as soon as they're available. What happened with the CMV test?"

"It was negative, as we expected. We got a toxoplasmosis screen too, but it was negative as well," Newton answered.

"Well, at least we looked. I checked Mrs. Smith's chart, and she wasn't a smoker either. I hope I've helped you. Do you want me to do a deposition?" Dobbins asked.

"Yes. It will probably be in the next two or three weeks. I'll let you know. Will you be in town?"

"Yes, I should be, but please give me as much notice as you can so I can schedule coverage in the NICU."

"I will. I'll get the CT results to you as soon as I can. Thanks for helping. I'll be in touch." Newton left somewhat encouraged.

After the gastrostomy tube was inserted, Will was ready to go home. Angie went to get him, with Wilma, but only after considerable urging by Dr. Thomas. She was clearly not happy at the idea, refusing to talk to anyone unless forced. She paid scant attention to any of the instructions, leaving that for Wilma, and she barely glanced at Will as they took him out. At home, she sat hunched over in the family room while Wilma took the baby upstairs and arranged everything in the nursery. Angie was completely washed out by the trip to and from the hospital, and she felt as devoid of feeling and energy as the baby looked.

Angie was annoyed that she had to leave the office on what was supposed to be her first full day at work. Finally, she went up to the nursery and looked through the door, but she did not enter. She told Wilma she had to return to work and left. At work, she huddled in her chair, completely silent. She returned home at five to resume sitting in the family room.

Bill arrived home after six, rushed through the door to the family room, and went to Angie.

"So, how was your first full day of work? You'll be a great chief of the training division."

"I'm surprised you even have to ask, Bill," she glared at him. "In fact, I'm really annoyed with you. Did you try to call me? Did you come see me when you were at the office? You don't pay any attention to me at all. The hospital insisted on discharging Will today, and they asked that one of us be there. They needed the bed so he had to come home a day earlier than planned. It was a very depressing experience, and I almost couldn't go back to the office this afternoon. Thank God for Wilma. She took care of everything." Exhausted, she sagged in her chair.

Bill backed away.

"Angie, that's not fair. I had no idea that the baby was coming home. Why didn't you call me and give me a chance? I would have tried to be there, at least when you got home. You knew this morning that I planned a visit to a law firm that's almost seventy-five miles from here. It turned out to be a much larger deal than we had anticipated, so I was tied up much longer than I expected."

"I did call when I got back to the office, but you weren't there." Angie's voice softened. "I'm sorry, honey. I'm just upset."

"How is Will?"

"Come on, and I'll show you. Nothing's changed, except that he's here and that he'll need constant attention. Wilma can do most of it, but we'll have to have more help to give her some time off. I called the service to arrange it." Angie led him toward the stairs.

The nursery had been next to their bedroom, but because there had to be a full-time nurse or attendant, they'd moved it to the other end of the second floor to give themselves and the nurses more privacy. The new nursery was right above the kitchen by the back stairs. They slowly approached the door.

"Do you see, Bill? He just lies there. We have to move him every hour, and when we touch him, he gets spastic. All his feedings go through that tube in his stomach, and he drools all the time. The doctors say he can't swallow very well, and they don't think he ever will. They're worried that he'll get pneumonia because he could choke and some of that stuff could get into his lungs."

"Angie, we have, or we'll get, the best medical help there is. If anything can be done for him, it will be. You know I'm just as unhappy as you are. You've never asked me about all the dreams I had for our son, his growing up, learning baseball and football, going camping, and all the rest. All of that is ruined forever, I'm afraid."

"I'm sorry, Bill. This has been one hell of a day. Just come hold me."

"Angie," he said after a moment, "I think we really need to get some professional help. Please think about it."

"No, thanks, Bill. The only thing I want right now is to win this suit." She was vehement.

"So do I, Angie, but we still have to develop a future for ourselves. You've been unwilling to think or talk about anything but revenge. We've got to build our lives on something more solid. Please come with me to see someone?"

"Bill, no. Please don't bring it up again."

"Okay," he answered reluctantly.

After the baby came home, Bill and Angie were assaulted every hour at home by the noise of the suction machine to keep Will's airway clear. He cried after each episode, another shrill reminder of his deficits. Wilma and the other nurses provided all the care, and Angie and Bill made one or, at the most, two visits a day.

18

Janet didn't sleep at all the night before her deposition, and spent some of it pacing in the study. She tried to read notes she had gotten from Newton, but she couldn't concentrate. Finally, she brewed a pot of strong coffee and tried to calm herself by reading the paper and petting Jenny. A shower helped, but breakfast with Mike was silent. Then she dragged herself to the garage to go to the hospital.

Janet met with Clark for a few minutes alone.

"Kline usually dresses and acts as if he were arguing a case in front of the United States Supreme Court. Jones is usually more casual, and he'll have papers scattered all over the place before we're finished."

"Clark, which one do I need to worry about?"

"Both of them, but especially Jones. He'll sneak up on you."

"Oh, boy. Just what I wanted to hear."

"Dr. Jankowski, this is Herbert Kline and Jefferson Jones, who represent Mr. and Mrs. Smith. They'll be asking most of the questions. I'm not sure if you've met Chester House for the university," Newton said.

She nodded hello and shook hands with each of them.

"Have you ever given a deposition before?" Newton asked.

"No. This is my first." Janet was pale, but seemingly calm.

"The purpose of this deposition is to get the facts surrounding the birth of William N. Smith, Jr. on record. It's called discovery. I'll be right here if there are any questions. I think we can begin."

The deposition was conducted in Newton's conference room this time. Unlike Kline's conference room or Segal's office, Newton's could be best described as hospital functional. The table and chairs were metal and worn. The walls were lined with metal shelves, filled haphazardly with piles of papers and some bound records. The only picture was of the hospital. Everyone present sat facing each other, except the court reporter who was in a corner.

"Do you swear to tell the truth, the whole truth, and nothing but the truth?" the court reporter asked.

"I do."

"Please state your full name," Kline said.

"Janet S. Jankowski is my professional name. Is that what you want to know?" Janet was wearing a very attractive navy suit and a white blouse. At Newton's urging, she had put on makeup, earrings, and a string of pearls. That, combined with her ten-pound weight loss, made her look better than usual. She hoped her feeling of terror wouldn't betray her.

"Yes, but now tell us your married name."

"Janet J. Johnson."

"Are you a resident of this city?"

"Yes."

"How long have you lived here?"

"Since I started medical school, nineteen years ago."

"Where did you go to college?"

"At Vanderbilt University in Nashville, Tennessee."

"You said you went to medical school here in St. Louis. Which school?"

"Missouri State Medical School."

"When did you graduate from medical school?"

"I graduated fifteen years ago."

148

"Are you a medical doctor, an M.D.?"

"Yes, that's correct."

"You're married. Where and when did you meet your husband?"

"In our freshman year in medical school. We sat next to each other in lab classes."

"When did you marry?"

"Between the second and third years."

"Did he specialize after medical school?"

"Yes. He did a three-year residency in internal medicine, and then he did two more years to specialize in cardiology, all at the medical school. He's board certified in both."

"Does he practice here?"

"Yes. He's on the staff at Memorial."

"Where did you do your residency?"

"I did my residency in obstetrics and gynecology at University Hospital, finishing eleven years ago."

"Are you board certified?"

"Yes, I was certified two years later."

"Are you licensed in Missouri?"

"Yes."

"Dr. Jankowski's curriculum vitae is submitted to be attached to the deposition," Newton added.

"Thank you. How many talks do you give a year on medical topics?" Kline had a long list of prepared questions, which he and Jones shared, and on which Jones wrote occasional notes.

"Three or four I suppose."

"Where, if I may ask?"

"At Memorial Hospital, either to our OB-GYN staff or to the OB-GYN nurses."

"Is that typical of someone in private practice?"

"It's typical for the staff at Memorial. I have no way of judging other places, but I'd guess so."

"How many meetings do you attend a year?"

"Three or four."

"Where?"

"I usually go to one national, one regional, and a couple of local meetings, plus the St. Louis Gynecological Society meetings six or eight times a year. My husband is a cardiologist, and we go together when they're out of town. We try to find meetings, in either cardiology or OB-GYN, that have topics of interest for both of us."

"Do you feel you qualify as an expert?"

Newton objected.

"We established Dr. Jankowski's credentials as a specialist."

"Our experts were examined intensely. I'm trying to establish where Dr. Jankowski fits in," refuted Kline.

"Dr. Jankowski, I'm instructing you not to answer the question. Mr. Kline, Dr. Jankowski is a highly qualified practitioner of obstetrics and gynecology. She is the defendant in this case, and she does not have to establish herself as an expert in the sense that witnesses for either side who are brought in as experts do. I'm surprised at this line of questioning." Newton's face reddened.

Jones put his hand on Kline's arm, as if to restrain him.

"Withdrawn," surrendered Kline. "Dr. Jankowski, have you practiced here at Memorial Hospital since you finished residency?"

"For ten years. I was on the faculty at the university for one year after that."

"Why did you spend only one year at the university?"

"When I finished my residency, my husband still had one more year to complete his fellowship in cardiology. We weren't certain where we wanted to go when he finished, so I needed a job for that year. The OB-GYN chairman was nice enough to give me a job, even though he knew I probably would leave at the end of one year."

"Did you look at other communities?"

"Yes. We seriously considered going to St. Luke's Hospital in Kansas City, Missouri. I guess inertia kept us here."

"That still doesn't answer why you left the university."

"I really wanted private practice. I enjoyed the year at the medical school, but I didn't want to worry about getting grants, writing papers, and all the rest that's part of academic practice. I just wanted to take care of patients in my own practice."

"Is this your first professional liability suit?"

"Objection."

"We can argue that in front of the judge," Kline said.

"You may answer the question," conceded Newton.

"Yes."

"Does that mean that this is the first bad baby you've had?"

"Objection."

"I'll withdraw the question," Kline gave in. "Dr. Jankowski, you may refer to the records if you wish. Was Mrs. Smith's pregnancy normal?"

"Yes, quite normal."

Janet continued to look fine, but inside, she was as tight as a coiled spring. There was an occasional tremor in her voice, and she hesitated some in answering. Her resolve was strong, and the toughness Mike knew well still remained. Without doubt, her fear about the deposition was reinforced by the sharpness of the questions and the interchanges between the lawyers.

"Would you please go into more detail?"

"Mrs. Smith and her husband were seen early, at about six weeks of pregnancy, and she was seen regularly after that. Mr. Smith came with her every time, I think. There were no problems other than morning sickness. They had come in about three months before attempting to get pregnant to be counseled about the right things to do."

"Mrs. Smith is considered old to be having babies, isn't that right?"

"Not any more, but we did give her special tests because she is past thirty-five."

"And what were those tests?"

"She had an amniocentesis at twelve to thirteen weeks to determine if the baby was genetically normal."

"Was it?"

"Yes."

"Isn't there another test, chorionic villus sampling, CVS, which can be done much earlier?"

"Yes, a little earlier."

"Why wasn't that done?"

"Mrs. Smith had enough nausea and vomiting that we thought it was probably better not to add the stress of CVS."

"Do you consider that degree of nausea and vomiting normal?"

"Yes. It happens once in a while."

"Did you give her something for the nausea?"

"No. There isn't anything approved for nausea in pregnancy unless the mother is so sick she has to be hospitalized, and then there still isn't much we can do other than give her IV fluids."

"Why is that?"

"Becuase of too many lawsuits against the makers of the antinausea drugs by greedy lawyers and plaintiffs."

"Objection." Kline looked at Newton.

"Can you re-word that statement a little?" Newton asked Dr. Jankowski.

"No. In my opinion, I stated the truth."

"The objection stands," Kline said.

"We'll discuss it with the judge. Please continue," Newton sighed.

Janet smiled slightly.

"Was any further testing done during the pregnancy?" Kline asked.

"Yes. At about eighteen weeks, we did another ultrasound to be sure that the baby was structurally normal, which it was."

"Can you tell the sex of the baby by these tests?"

"Yes. It was a boy. The amniocentesis proved that."

"Did you tell Mrs. Smith?"

"Yes. She wanted to know, and they both seemed to be thrilled."

"Was any further testing done beyond that?"

"No, only routine blood and urine tests. Her pregnancy was entirely normal."

"Did you do a nonstress test?"

"No. I didn't see any reason to do one. As I've said, this pregnancy was uncomplicated."

"Doesn't her age make a difference?"

"If she were high risk in any other way, I would have. By itself, age wasn't enough."

"How about a contraction stress test?"

"Same answer. It wasn't indicated."

"Would either of them have shown anything, if you had done them?"

"Probably not. They don't last long enough. It took at least two hours of regular contractions to cause the first dip. Those tests are rarely longer than an hour."

"Did you do an ultrasound exam late in pregnancy?"

"Actually, I did. It's reported in the chart as 'AFI normal.' "

"Did you do any other tests?"

"No. Her pregnancy was quite normal, as I've said."

"Did Mrs. Smith go into labor by herself?"

"Yes. She began to have contractions in the afternoon of her due date. Her water broke at about six o'clock, and she came to the hospital as instructed."

"Were you there when she came in?"

"Yes. I had asked her to call me if anything happened, which she did, and I met her at the hospital."

"It sounds like you were worried about something."

"Mr. Kline, I always try to meet my patients at the hospital. I resent your attitude."

Kline objected to this remark as well.

"We'll agree to withdraw the statement about attitude," said Newton.

Then, Kline and Jones switched roles, their routine for most depositions.

"Did you examine Mrs. Smith when she came in?" Jones asked after a brief moment.

"Yes. She had ruptured her membranes and was in early labor. Her cervix was three centimeters dilated and completely thinned out. The baby's head was in her pelvis. Her contractions were every five minutes, and they were forty seconds long."

"Did you do anything else?"

"Yes. We attached an external fetal monitor and a labor monitor to her abdomen."

"Why did you do that?"

"The fetal monitor was hooked up to make sure that the baby's heart rate was normal, which it was, and the labor monitor was hooked up to make sure that Mrs. Smith was having regular contractions and that they were getting stronger, which they were."

"Was anything else done?"

"Yes. We put in a catheter for epidural anesthesia."

"Please explain that."

"It's done by the anesthesiologist. A small plastic tube is put through a needle into the space inside the spinal canal in the lower back, but outside the membrane covering the spinal cord."

"Was anything injected?"

"Yes, the anesthesiologist injected a small amount of local

anesthesia to be sure that the catheter was working properly."

"Did anything else happen at that time?"

"We started an IV."

"Why?"

"It's pretty routine to start an IV when an epidural is used."

"Why?"

"One of the complications for a mother having an epidural is a possible drop in blood pressure. The IV is used to help maintain a normal blood pressure."

"Did it drop?"

"The blood pressure?"

"Yes."

"No."

"What happened after that?"

"We waited for labor to pick up by itself."

"Did it?"

"Yes. Mrs. Smith had fairly rapid progress and was given anesthesia when she was four to five centimeters along."

"You're talking about dilation, I assume?"

"Yes."

"Why was more anesthesia given then?"

"Because Mrs. Smith and her husband requested it. Both the anesthesiologist and I thought that it would help her labor by providing pain relief and by helping her relax."

"Were there any problems?"

"No. Her blood pressure remained normal throughout. So did the fetal heart tones, the heart rate."

"So, you don't think that the anesthesia had anything to do with what happened later?"

"No, I do not."

"Was anything else done then?"

"We put on the fetal scalp electrode and the internal pressure monitor."

"When did anything happen that was out of the ordinary?"

"There was a severe drop in heart rate at six to seven centimeters dilation."

"What did you do about it?"

"We increased the IV fluids, turned Mrs. Smith on her left side, gave her nasal oxygen, and watched the tracing."

"Why did you do that?"

"The extra IV fluids are given to make sure that there is enough blood volume to maintain circulation to the uterus and placenta. The oxygen is given to make sure that there is enough available for the baby. Turning her to her left side prevents the pooling of blood in her pelvis and legs so that there is plenty for her heart to pump to the uterus."

"What happened?"

"The heart rate came back to perfectly normal after about two and a half minutes."

"Did you do anything else?"

"We decided not to inject any more epidural anesthesic."

"Why?"

"Even though we had no evidence to think that anesthesia was the cause, we decided to be cautious and not take that chance."

"What did you do then?"

"We watched very carefully."

"Who is we?"

"Me, the nurse, and the resident."

"All of you?"

"Yes."

"Why didn't you do a cesarean section right then?"

"There wasn't any reason to."

"Do you mean that you didn't consider this drop in heart rate to be serious?"

"I didn't say that."

"What did you say?"

"The heart rate came back to normal with IV fluids, position change, and oxygen. There was even an acceleration. We watched to be sure it stayed normal. I told the nurses to be ready for a c-section if anything else happened. As I said before, we did not give more epidural anesthesia in case that was the cause. We were concerned."

"You don't think a cesarean section was necessary at that time?"

"No, I don't, even knowing what happened after that."

"What did happen next?" Kline took over again.

"The heart rate dropped again thirty minutes later, so we took her immediately to do a cesarean section. The baby was delivered in seventeen minutes from the beginning of that drop."

"Why did it take so long?"

"That's not long at all. It took almost two minutes to realize that the heart rate was staying down. Another few minutes were used unplugging the monitors and oxygen and moving her down the hall. That's as fast as we can do a section at Memorial."

"Why did you do a vertical incision from her umbilicus to her pubic bone? I thought bikini incisions were the routine today."

"It's much faster to do a vertical incision, and we were in a hurry. The Pfannestiel, or bikini, incision takes almost twice as long and doesn't provide as much room to get the baby out."

"Isn't it true that the bikini incision is stronger?"

"Yes, that's true, but it seems unimportant to me now. I'm sure she must have healed okay, or I would have heard about it."

"Don't you know?"

"No. Mrs. Smith didn't keep her postpartum appointment. She called to cancel and said that she was okay. I haven't seen her since she left the hospital."

"Did she see someone else, another OB?"

"I don't know, but I rather doubt it. We didn't get a request to send her records to another OB."

Jones made a note to ask Angie.

"What anesthesia was used for the cesarean section?"

"General. She was put to sleep. We had not reinjected the epidural as I already testified, and I didn't want to wait for it since it would have been slower than general anesthesia."

"Was Mrs. Smith okay?"

"What do you mean?"

"Was she okay after the section?"

"Yes. The cesarean section went very smoothly, and she had less than the usual blood loss, about six hundred milliliters."

"Did she recover from the anesthesia okay?"

"Yes. She did quite well."

"How was the baby?"

"As you know, the baby was quite depressed at birth. He had a feeble cry and no muscle tone. His heart rate and breathing were barely acceptable."

"Were the pediatricians there?"

"Yes, and they took over management of the baby. The pediatricians come to every section at Memorial."

"Do you still persist in your belief that a cesarean section after the first drop in heart rate would not have ended in a better result?"

"Objection, she has already answered that question."

"Mr. Newton, I'd like her to answer it anyway."

"Go ahead, Dr. Jankowski."

"Mr. Kline, my belief that my treatment was proper at that time is even stronger now than it was then. This baby has CP. All the studies we now have indicate that CP is caused before the onset of labor. I could not have made this baby normal. It was already too late."

"That's all I have," said Kline.

"I have a few questions," Newton indicated. "You stated earlier that the Smiths seemed thrilled with the results of the genetic testing. Please explain."

"They were excited by the news that they were having a boy and that he was genetically normal. Mrs. Smith had told me that they couldn't tolerate having an abnormal child."

"When did you learn that?"

"When we discussed the reasons for doing the genetic testing. They were adamant about it."

"If you will look at the heart rate tracing, there's some lack of beat-to-beat variability, beginning when Mrs. Smith had just entered the hospital."

"That's correct. We thought it either represented a sleep cycle or the epidural or both. Beat-to-beat variability does not show up as well on external monitors. That's one of the reasons I put in the internal monitor when the epidural was injected. It confirmed the lack of beat-to-beat variability, which we explained then as I already indicated. But it was worrisome enough that I sat with her throughout her labor. In retrospect, it represented the damage done by something before labor that had already caused the CP."

"So, you do know that lack of beat-to-beat variability may be abnormal?"

"Yes, and it helped us make the decision to go right to a cesarean section when the second drop in heart rate occurred. If the first drop hadn't come back up, we would have done something then."

"What is your cesarean section rate?"

"Objection," said Kline.

"Counselor, we asked Dr. Segal the same question. I think it's appropriate here as well."

"I may wish to ask further questions then."

"That's fine," Newton persisted. "Answer the question, please, Dr. Jankowski."

"It's about twenty-one percent."

"Can you be more specific?"

"No. It varies year to year, and in an individual practice, one section makes a difference."

"What is the section rate at Memorial Hospital?"

"Last year it was twenty-point-five percent. That's the year Mrs. Smith delivered."

"Your rate, if anything, is slightly higher."

"Yes, but I doubt that the difference is significant."

"You sent the placenta to pathology. Is that common practice?"

"Yes. We do that anytime something out of the ordinary happens."

"What did they find?"

"Pathology hasn't given a final diagnosis yet. I believe they found some nonspecific endarteritis. I understand they sent samples to outside experts for consultation."

"Explain endarteritis please."

"It's the inflammation of the terminal arteries right before they enter the capillaries."

"What can cause this change?"

"Preeclampsia, viral infections, or a lot of other things. That's why it's called nonspecific."

"Did Mrs. Smith have any of those things?"

"No, she didn't. I think that's why they sent samples to outside experts. I don't know when the results will be back."

"That's all I have," Newton announced.

Kline began questioning again.

"Many private hospitals in this city and country have higher section rates. Does that bother you?"

"No. The University Hospital rate runs less than Memorial. I think that's a pretty good standard, since they have more high-risk patients who are likely to need sections. The ACOG is trying to lower the national rate to something similar to ours from the current twenty-three percent."

"Define ACOG."

"American College of Obstetricians and Gynecologists."

"I'll ask again. Isn't your personal rate a little low compared to other private hospitals? Maybe a higher rate by you would have resulted in a much earlier section for Mrs. Smith, with a better result."

"Objection," Newton interrupted.

"I won't withdraw this question. We can argue later. Please ask your client to answer."

Newton hesitated.

"Go ahead."

"My personal rate is not too low. And more importantly, as I've testified before, this baby was abnormal before the onset of labor. Nothing I could have done in the hospital would or could have made a difference. Finally, accepted practice dictated the wait when the first drop in heart tones responded to treatment."

"Nothing further."

"Herb, Clark keeps bringing up the beat-to-beat variability. What does he have going there that we aren't anticipating?" Jones asked when they returned to their office.

"I don't know." Kline leaned back in his chair. "As you already know, Segal and Thomas assure us that there's nothing to worry about, that it's just a normal variation. I sure hope they're correct."

"Me, too. The whole case rests on that premise. I know you don't want to change focus at this late date, but maybe we should spend more time looking at her prenatal care. This placenta thing might be important. There might be something there that could explain the CP," Jones suggested.

"I'll do that," Kline answered.

"On top of everything else, I hope we don't hear too much more about section rates. Segal and his hospital are way out of line, and we're likely to get beat up on that issue. Dr. Jankowski may be in her first lawsuit, but she handled herself pretty well once things got going. Maybe we should talk to another maternal-fetal person?" queried Jones.

"I'd rather not, Jefferson, if we can avoid it. The two experts we have are so darned expensive that I think the Smiths would rebel if we went for another. Plus, it would hold us back several months. Let's see what Clark's expert, Dr. Workman, has to say first," Kline suggested.

"Okay. When is she scheduled for deposition?"

"Next week. After that, we'll depose Wilma James, as a witness to the turmoil in Mr. and Mrs. Smith's lives. Ordinarily, I would save her for trial, but I'm hoping her testimony will help force a settlement. I think Clark has a neonatologist, a Dr. Dobbins, too. That should wind it up, and then maybe we can start negotiating or get a trial date set," Kline answered.

"Janet, you did very well in the deposition today," Newton congratulated her. "I know you were scared, but you got stronger as the questions went on."

"Thanks. I just hope I never have to do it again," she responded.

"With luck, you won't, even in a trial for this case. The beat-to-beat variability issue and the section rates issue are hurting them. Stick with me on this."

They chatted about the details for a few minutes.

"Don't worry about me," Janet answered. "I don't want to lose."

She pulled herself together and drove to her office for an afternoon of patients. Once there, she made a quick call to Mike to let him know she had survived.

162

Janet finished at her office at five o'clock and made rounds at the hospital, which were brief because of all the cutbacks she had been required to make. She was home at six o'clock, in time for dinner.

Carol and Michael were bubbling with enthusiasm, as usual.

"Mom, can I ask—"

"May I, please, Michael," Mike interrupted.

"Mom, may I please ask Jimmy to sleep over Friday night? We can stay up in my room so we won't be in the way."

Janet didn't respond.

"Mom, may I, please?"

"Michael, it's okay with me if your father agrees," Janet answered irritably.

"Sure, Michael," Mike quickly responded. "Ask his mother to bring him over after school. We'll get pizza, and you guys can have a picnic up there. Promise not to make a mess."

"We won't, Dad. Thanks."

"Dad, I want to go to Sara's house if they're going to be here," Carol pronounced indignantly.

"That's fine, honey. Just let me know."

Michael started to respond, but a look from his father silenced him.

The remainder of dinner was quiet. Janet just stared at her plate.

Later that evening, Janet talked to Mike at length.

"The deposition was really awful. I don't think I can face having to go to trial. It will just be worse." Janet's stomach was still upset, and she looked pale and tired. She had eaten almost nothing. "I think I did okay. At least that's what Clark said, but it sure tore me up inside."

"Honey, you have to remember that Kline and Jones have no

personal stake in this, other than their fee. To them, it's like a game. If they can get you mad enough to lose your temper, they may win because of some slip you make. That's the reason they pick on you. From what I hear, it's the same for anyone who's a defendant in a malpractice case. You're just learning the hard way."

"You can say that again. My big problem is that this is not the way I want to practice, having to worry about lawsuits all the time. And I don't want to give up all this time and have this much upset just because someone is unhappy with their baby. I lose, even if I win," she whispered.

"Janet, their baby is a disaster."

"Damn it, Mike, I know that, but they still shouldn't be able to file a lawsuit without being able to base their argument in medical fact. Even if I win, I can't recover all the lost time and income, and we won't ever get over what it's done to us and the kids. This is not why I decided to go to med school. This takes all the fun out of seeing patients, and once the fun's gone, there's no reason to continue."

"I hope you're not thinking of quitting."

"It's crossed my mind a number of times since this has started," she admitted. "We can get along just fine on your income if I quit. I'm sorry, but I'm getting pushed and shoved around right now, almost more than I can handle. I simply don't know how to manage anything, no matter how routine, and I don't see any hope for improvement. I'm desperate."

Mike tried to console her, but to no avail. He held her close until she became sleepy, and then he helped her up to bed.

Janet awakened in the middle of the night, terrified, imagining that she had closed herself in the garage and turned on the car. As she gained consciousness, she was certain that she could smell the exhaust fumes. Each time she awakened during the rest of the night, she could remember more details about how she had tried to kill herself in her dream. She was so upset the next morning that she couldn't even talk to Mike about it. *How could I even think of leaving Mike and the kids,* she thought, as she examined the circles under her eyes in the mirror.

Janet cancelled her morning office appointments, and she stayed with the children until they went to school. Then she took a long hot bath and tried to get her thoughts back in order. She didn't think she would do anything foolish, but she was really frightened and distressed that she'd even thought of suicide. Finally, she went to the office to catch up on some paperwork and reading. Darlene had kept the afternoon light, so she wasn't rushed. By the end of the day, she had recovered some of her composure.

The day after Janet's deposition, Kline called Angie.

"According to Dr. Jankowski, you haven't been back for a postpartum checkup. Is that true?"

"Yes. I just couldn't face her after what she did to us."

"Did you try anyone else?"

"Yes, but I couldn't get in."

"Why is that?"

"They didn't have appointments for a new patient for several weeks, and the times weren't very convenient."

"How many OBs did you call?"

"Two."

"So you really didn't try very hard."

"No, I guess not."

"Mrs. Smith, I think it's important that you have a postpartum checkup, especially since you had a c-section. We need to know if you are all okay. I'll arrange an appointment for you with Dr. Segal in the next few days. He's our maternal-fetal expert, you may remember."

"Yes, I do remember. I really don't think it's necessary. I'm doing fine."

"Mrs. Smith, I insist."

"Oh, all right."

Angie saw Dr. Segal several days later. He tried to make an issue of the vertical incision, but otherwise she was fine.

Kline ignored the location of the incision.

Bill and Angie sat in their family room, neither able to concentrate on reading or TV. This was their usual behavior each evening, unless one of them had a meeting.

"Angie, we haven't been out or done anything since the baby was born. How about I take you to dinner tomorrow night? There's a new place I hear is pretty good."

"No thanks. I can't bear the idea of seeing someone who will ask about Will. I can't answer that question one more time. The people at the office are about to do me in. Everyone asks everyday. Some of them are even asking about the lawsuit." She grimaced at him.

"Angie, they're just trying to show some interest. I get the same thing, and I agree it's hard, but I think it would be worse if no one cared," Bill slowly responded.

"Maybe you're right, but that doesn't change my not wanting to go out."

"Then let's have somebody over here this weekend? It would do us both good to be with friends again."

"Bill, don't you realize that it would be even worse to have someone here wanting to go up to see him? I couldn't stand it."

"Angie, it isn't reasonable to keep on living like this. We've got to get back to normal. I still say we need to see a counselor."

"Bill, don't, please. Can't you understand my life has been ruined by that damn doctor? It's never going to be the same again."

"Angie, I'm just trying to hold things together. My life's been ruined just as much as yours has been, and we can't continue on like this. Please come with me to see someone."

"For the last time, no."

Bill had found a counselor by calling one of the groups dedicated to helping couples who have lost a baby. The group strongly suggested that both he and Angie go see the counselor together, and they had given several other suggestions. Even though he didn't want to go alone, Bill knew he had to get something started in the right direction.

19

"Dr. Workman, this is Herbert Kline and Jefferson Jones, who represent Mr. and Mrs. Smith. They will be doing most of the questioning today. I think you know Chester House. I assume you are familiar with depositions?" Newton asked. Kim had just come into Newton's conference room, on time, wearing her white coat.

"Unfortunately, yes, I am. Good morning. I think I met Mr. Kline and Mr. Jones a couple of years ago," Kim responded.

"Good morning," all of them answered.

"I think that's right," Jones added. "We did talk briefly about a case a couple of years ago. You advised us not to pursue it."

Kim remembered that they had ignored her advice and ultimately lost. Her pager sounded, so she excused herself to call her secretary to hold all pages.

"If there's no objection, let's begin," Newton suggested, when she was ready.

Kim was a little nervous because of her friendship with Janet and her desire to help her, even though she had given depositions on other cases several times before.

"Do you swear to tell the truth, the whole truth, and nothing but the truth?" asked the court reporter.

"I do."

"Please state your name," Kline said.

"Kimberly Workman."

"You are a medical doctor, an M.D.?"

"That's correct."

"Are you a resident of this city?"

"Yes."

"How long have you lived here?"

"Twenty-one years, except for two years in Boston."

"Where did you obtain your medical education?"

"I graduated from Missouri State Medical School seventeen years ago and then did a residency in obstetrics and gynecology at University Hospital, finishing thirteen years ago."

"Is that all your training?"

"No. I then did a two-year fellowship in maternal-fetal medicine, finishing eleven years ago. That was at Harvard Medical School and the Brigham and Women's Hospital."

"Are you licensed in Missouri?"

"Yes."

"Copies of Dr. Workman's curriculum vitae and bibliography are submitted," Newton stated.

"Are you certified by any board?"

"Yes. I'm certified in both basic obstetrics and gynecology and the subspecialty of maternal-fetal medicine by the American Board of Obstetrics and Gynecology."

"Were you successful the first time you took the exams?"

Newton objected.

"That's not relevant and is certainly very close to being insulting."

"The question stands. Since most of her training was done here, I need to find out how well-qualified she is. We can discuss this in front of the judge."

"Go ahead and answer," Newton instructed her, "but the objection still stands."

"Yes, I was. Were you?" Kim asked.

"Now, I object." Kline threw his hands up in the air.

"If you can't stand the heat, get out of the kitchen," Kim shot back at him.

"I hope you'll agree, Mr. Newton," Kline sputtered, "that

things are a little out of control here. At least, I think so. It was certainly not my intention to bring things down to this level. I withdraw the question."

Kim was clearly pleased at having nettled Kline, and she looked as if she wanted to continue badgering him. Actually, she was a little scared by her own bravado, and she knew the court reporter recorded everything, unless the opposing lawyers agreed to go off the record. It suited her just fine that Kline and Newton had regained control. She wanted to get the deposition over with. After some hesitation on his part, Kline resumed questioning.

"I note that you are chief or head of the Division of Maternal-Fetal Medicine. How long have you held that position?"

"I joined the division when I completed my fellowship and became head five years ago."

"Do you examine for the American Board for Obstetricians and Gynecologists?"

"It's the American Board of Obstetrics and Gynecology. I was an examiner for the basic board for two years. Then I became an examiner for the Maternal-Fetal Medicine Board six years ago. Last year, I was asked to be a member of the committee that supervises the exam."

"Thank you. I note in your bibliography that you are the author or co-author of seventy-seven papers. Did you really participate in the preparation of all of them?"

"Mr. Kline, your question is insulting and borders on slander." Kim looked at him square in the eye.

"Off the record," Kline stipulated, "Dr. Workman, I can ask the judge involved in this case to hold you in contempt of court if you do not stop this behavior now." He almost shouted at her.

"Mr. Kline," House interrupted, "I'm not so sure. You are charging Dr. Workman with unethical conduct by insinuating that she has attached her name to reports of studies in which she didn't participate. Because such behavior is the responsibility of the medical school and the university, you are inpugning them as well."

"Mr. Newton and Mr. House, I'm trying to assess the credibility of your witness."

"Herb, I think we can do it in a different way. Why don't we step outside for a minute?" Jones said. "Please excuse us."

"Herb, get a hold of yourself," Jones said, once they were outside. "This witness isn't that tough. As a matter of fact, if she doesn't control her mouth, we can use it to our advantage in court."

"Okay, Jefferson. I guess I'm just being too eager to discredit her. I'll try to find another way."

"Please. We don't want either Newton or House to gain an advantage from this."

"Kim, that's enough. You can't win this kind of battle. He has the right and duty to make you prove your credentials," Newton said when they were left alone. House agreed.

"I know. He just makes me mad, and I enjoy making him blow up," she answered, "but I'll behave."

Kline and Jones walked back into the room and sat down. Kline immediately resumed where he left off in the deposition.

"We're back on the record now. Please describe your involvement in the papers listed in your bibliography."

"I was principal investigator in most of them, or I directly supervised junior faculty or fellows. In a few of the early reports, I was in the position of being junior faculty or a fellow under the supervision of one of my sponsors or mentors. In all of these papers, I was directly involved."

"Thank you. What has been the primary area in which you've done research?"

"All but a couple of case reports from my residency days are in obstetrics rather than gynecology. My early research was in the general area of fetal and maternal physiology. For the past several years, my personal interest has been cerebral palsy, its causes and prevention."

"Are you considered an expert on this subject?"

"Yes, I am."

"How so?"

"I am asked to present lectures on cerebral palsy several times a year at major institutions, and research reports from my unit are regularly accepted for presentation at major meetings. In addition, my unit has received grants from several national and international agencies for research on cerebral palsy. Because research money is in short supply, we compete rather vigorously on a national, occasionally international, level for these awards."

"I assume you mean national rather than regional meetings?"

"Yes, but we also present at several international meetings each year."

"Who is we?"

"I have five faculty physicians certified in maternal-fetal medicine, two Ph.D.s, and four fellows working with me, plus two or three postdoctoral students working with the PhD.s. We have a very busy program.

"Do you personally attend all of these meetings?"

"No, probably only five or six a year, but I'm directly involved in everything that is presented by a representative of our group at any of these meetings."

Newton interrupted.

"We can arrange testimony attesting to Dr. Workman's expertise if that will be helpful."

"That won't be necessary," Kline answered.

Jones nudged Kline and pushed the legal pad to him. Then he began questioning Kim.

"Are you familiar with the Smith case, the one under question here?"

"Yes."

"Were you involved in her care?"

"No."

"Then how are you familiar with the case?"

"In three ways. First, I have carefully reviewed all the records. Second, her case was presented at one of our three-times-a-week conferences right after the baby was born, so I had heard about it even before I reviewed the records. Finally, I have discussed the case with Dr. Jankowski."

"But you were not involved directly in her care."

"As I already stated, I was not. I did not hear about Mrs. Smith until after the fact."

"What fact do you mean?"

"Birth."

"The allegation has been made that there was a delay in responding to the drop in fetal heart rate and that the delay is responsible for causing the cerebral palsy and possible mental retardation the baby now has."

"Is that a question?"

"How do you respond to that allegation?"

"I think it is dead wrong."

"Will you please tell me what you think did happen?"

"No one can know for sure, at least so far. However, I think something was wrong with this baby before labor ever started, as evidenced by the lack of variability in the heart rate from the time she came in. This fits with what we know about cerebral palsy, which isn't very much. At least ninety-five percent of babies born with CP develop it before labor begins. It is rare to have an insult to a baby during labor that is severe enough to cause CP that the

173

baby can survive, especially at term, which this baby was. When I look at this record, I don't see any evidence of such an insult. There wasn't even any meconium in the amniotic fluid."

"What does that mean?"

"Meconium is the contents of the baby's colon. The baby passes meconium when it is stressed by low oxygen, low blood flow, low blood pressure, or something similar. It may be thin and discolor the fluid, which indicates old insult, or it may be thick, which means an insult in the preceding few minutes. But there wasn't any meconium in the amniotic fluid in this case."

"Please continue with what you think did happen."

It was familiar territory for Kim, just like being in a classroom.

"There wasn't any bleeding, there wasn't a loop of cord around the baby's neck, and the cord wasn't caught in front of a shoulder or anywhere else. There wasn't a knot in the cord. There was no chance for pushing or an accident in the second stage of labor. Finally, there wasn't a problem with the anesthesia, either the epidural or the general. In summary, I think this baby had damage, whatever caused it, before labor began."

"How can you look at this tracing and say that the first dip in heart tones is not important?"

"I didn't say that. The first drop in heart rate, which was severe, is important. It came without warning and without any apparent cause. I think it represents a damaged brain that occurred before labor. Because of the already existing damage, the baby responded to the stress of normal labor with a severe drop in heart rate."

"How do you explain the second drop?"

"I haven't finished with the first. I think the baby's heart rate came back to normal because of the oxygen, IV, and position change. Now we get to the second drop. This time, the continuation of normal labor, even with oxygen and the IV, was too stress-

174

ful for the baby to tolerate, so the second drop happened, and this time it stayed down."

"Wouldn't a rapid and prompt cesarean section have helped this baby?"

"No. A cesarean section right after the first drop would have had the same result. A cesarean section before the onset of labor would not have made any difference. This baby was already damaged."

"How can you prove that?"

"I can't. However, data on CP, much of it from our own unit, suggest that its origin in virtually every case is sometime in the sixth or seventh month of pregnancy, when the baby's brain is not mature enough to withstand the insult, whatever it is, but is mature enough for the baby not to die. We do know that fetal monitoring has not changed the incidence of CP, no matter how sophisticated the reader of the tracing. Adding all of that together, it is my opinion that this baby was already damaged and that cesarean section at any time around labor would not have helped. As a matter of fact, I certainly agree with the decision to do the section when it was done. Had it been done any later, the baby would have died."

"You do not agree with the opinion that an earlier section would have produced a normal baby?"

"Absolutely not."

"Mr. Kline, do you have anything further?"

"Nothing."

"I have a few questions," said Newton. "Dr. Workman, what is the cesarean section rate at University Hospital?"

"It varies between eighteen percent and nineteen percent. Right now, it is eighteen percent for the year that just ended. We would like to lower it to sixteen percent or seventeen percent."

"What is the national rate?"

"I understand it's somewhat higher, around twenty-three percent."

"How do you explain that difference?"

"It's not easy, but we think that it's because doctors in teaching hospitals, especially university programs, are less likely to be sued because they are considered to be experts."

"Please expound on that."

"Well, plaintiff lawyers seem to have less success against us. For that reason, we are more likely to go by the book."

"Do you mean that doctors in private nonteaching hospitals don't always go by the book?"

"No, but they might feel that they are more susceptible to lawsuits and, therefore, are more likely to do a section, feeling that doing so reduces their exposure. It's obvious they follow the book pretty closely, or they would have much higher rates."

"Are the results better in those hospitals?"

"No."

"The placenta apparently had some nonspecific endarteritis, and samples were sent to outside experts. What do you make of that?"

"Some nonspecific changes were found as you said. Specimens were sent to Michigan State and Penn State for review by national experts. They are pretty busy, so I'm not sure when we'll hear from them. To answer your question, I'm not sure what these changes mean. Mrs. Smith didn't have any of the usual diseases associated with these changes. The only things I can think of are a virus or some toxin we wouldn't expect. We'll wait for the experts and then look some more."

"That's all I have."

Back at their office, Jones unloaded.

"Herb, she really beat up on us. We have two absolutely opposing opinions, hers and Segal's, and I'm worried that she is the more believable witness. We may have some trouble with a jury, especially since Segal and Thomas come across as too slick.

And this section rate thing is getting difficult." He banged his fist on the desk.

"I know it. We'll have to coach both Segal and Thomas if they'll let us. This case is turning out to be much tougher than I had anticipated," Kline said gloomily.

"When's our next deposition on this one?" Jones asked.

"There's only one more for us, Wilma James. She'll turn out to be crucial because we'll need jury sympathy to help with the agony the Smiths have had. We'll get to her next week. Clark has one deposition scheduled, with a neonatologist named Alexander Dobbins. I think he plans to do it right after Wilma James."

"We'd better go through this whole case again. I'm still not convinced we aren't going to need another maternal-fetal expert to really nail this down. Do you have anyone in mind?"

"No, but maybe we'd better explore our options a little. Will you do that?"

"Sure," Jones answered.

"Kim, that was terrific. I think you shook them up a lot. I hope we can do as well with a jury if we have to go to trial," Newton said.

"Thanks," Kim answered. "I want to win this one very much for Janet."

"I agree. Where do you think we should go next on this?" Newton asked.

"I'd really like to see the CT results. It was done yesterday, I think. We should get them in a day or so. Anyway, I'm curious. Why did you ask me about section rates?"

"Segal's hospital has a thirty-five percent rate."

"You're kidding? If that's true, the Gyn Society, the Health Department, the hospital association, or someone needs to look into it. That's way out of line," Kim exclaimed.

177

"Segal testified to it in his deposition. You should have seen Kline squirm at that one."

"I'll bet he did. Let me know about the CT."

"I'll be in touch."

Newton met with his risk management committee two days later, on Friday.

"We had the deposition of our first expert Wednesday, Kim Workman. She did very well." He explained some of the details. "As you know, Janet's deposition went very well also. We have one more, Dr. Alexander Dobbins, which should put us in pretty good shape."

The committee seemed relieved.

"I think Kline has one deposition left, with the nurse who has been staying with the Smiths. Her name is Wilma James. I've never heard of her, so I don't think she does legal work for a living. I think he's using her to back up the mental turmoil part of the claim. I'll let you know. If anyone has comments or suggestions, I'd appreciate them now, or anytime."

None of the committee had anything more to offer.

"Even though Janet and Kim did well, we can't relax. Thomas and Segal are effective, and the nurse may be also. Trials are never a sure thing, especially bad baby trials." Newton ended with the meeting on that somber note, which did little for Janet's mood.

Mike walked into the family room that evening and found Janet huddled up in a chair.

"How are you holding up, honey?"

"About the same, I guess. At least I'm no worse. Kim was a big help, and the committee seems to think that her deposition, and mine, went well, even if I'm not so sure. Thank God, it's almost over," she sighed.

"I agree with that. We could use a little order in our lives."

Janet resumed her blank look, not responding to Mike's continued attempts at conversation. In fact, she had to be called several times to come to the dinner table.

After dinner, Janet retreated to the study, where she put a medical journal on her lap. She couldn't focus her eyes or brain on the writing, and she soon nodded off. After a couple of hours, Mike pushed her up to bed.

Janet didn't have any dreams that night, but when she awakened Saturday morning, the thoughts of suicide returned and remained with her all weekend.

On Monday, at the office, she found herself looking in the drug cabinet and thinking of taking an overdose of sleeping pills. She wondered if she should reconsider counseling, or even a psychiatrist, but she couldn't think clearly enough to make a decision.

"Dr. Jankowski, are you still here? The last patient left forty-five minutes ago." Nancy was alarmed on Monday evening to find Janet huddled in her chair, almost unresponsive. "Come on, let's get you up and out of here."

Janet looked up uncomprehendingly and then seemed to shake herself awake.

"I'm okay, Nancy. Thanks, though."

"Come on. I'll walk you to your car."

"You don't need to do that. Why are you still here, anyway?"

"I had some last minute paperwork to do, and I wanted to check in on you. I noticed a light under your door."

"Thanks, again," Janet responded grimly as she got into her car.

Nancy followed her home to make sure she got there safely. The next morning, she called Mike at his office.

"I'm glad you called, Nancy. She is seriously depressed.

Please watch her for me, and let's stay in touch every day."

"Okay, Dr. Johnson." Nancy, unsure why she did so, decided to look in the locked drug cabinet. Nothing was missing, but it had been rearranged, and only she and Janet had keys. She called to inform Mike later that day, and she doubled her vigilance.

20

Dobbins called Newton on Tuesday afternoon.

"My mother broke her hip this morning. She's in the operating room right now. I need to be there to help close her apartment and move her to an assisted care facility when she leaves the hospital. I hope I won't be gone more than two weeks, but I won't know until I'm there. Anyway, can you schedule my deposition for tomorrow?"

"I'll try. I'll call you back to confirm. Let's plan on tomorrow morning. I'll call Kline right now," Newton said. "And I'm sorry to hear about your mother."

"Thanks, Mr. Newton. I'll make plane reservations for the late afternoon."

Dobbins's deposition was scheduled at nine o'clock the next morning in Newton's conference room.

"Dr. Dobbins, this is Herbert Kline and Jefferson Jones. They represent Mr. and Mrs. Smith and will be doing most of the questioning today. I assume you are familiar with depositions?" Newton asked.

"Yes, I am, and I thank you for taking me out of order and in a hurry. As you know, something personal came up that makes me unavailable for the next couple of weeks. I'm leaving this afternoon." Dobbins looked his age, fifty-nine. A tweed jacket over tan slacks and his bow tie complemented his natural dignity and reserve. He sat calmly, apparently unruffled by the lawyers.

"We understand," Kline answered. "Let's begin."

"Do you swear to tell the truth, the whole truth, and nothing but the truth?" asked the court reporter.

"I do."

"Please state your name." Jones began this time around.

"Alexander Dobbins."

"Are you a resident of this city?"

"Yes, I am."

"Are you a medical doctor, an M.D.?"

"Yes, I am."

"Where did you obtain your medical education?"

"At Yale University Medical School. I graduated in 1959."

"And where did you receive your pediatric training?"

"At Yale, finishing three years later."

"Have you had any further training?"

"I spent the next two years as a pediatrician in the United States Air Force. I was stationed in California. Then I did a two-year fellowship in neonatology in London, England."

"Are you board certified?"

"Yes, in both pediatrics and in neonatology."

"Are you licensed in Missouri?"

"Yes."

"Here is his curriculum vitae to attach to the record," Newton added, as routine.

"Thank you." Kline and Jones took a few minutes to review the document. "Dr. Dobbins, you have published only twelve papers and none in the past several years. Why is that?" Jones asked.

"I realized early on that my strengths were in clinical care rather than in research. That's why I chose a private hospital rather than the medical school."

"If you don't mind, how then do you qualify as an expert?"

"I don't mind. My training and experience are outlined in my curriculum vitae. I won't repeat them. There is one minor inaccuracy, in that I've just been appointed as Clinical Associate Professor of Pediatrics at the medical school. That's not in my curriculum vitae yet. I now have students and residents rotating from there to my unit. We're considering rotating fellows as well. I believe I am considered to be a pretty good teacher and practitioner of neonatology."

"Be careful, Jefferson. Switch to something else," Kline interrupted in a whisper.

"Do you practice here in the city?"

"Yes, at Seacroft Hospital, where I'm head of the NICU."

"Just for the record, NICU means Neonatal Intensive Care Unit. I think I'm correct."

"That's right."

"Do you have other neonatologists working with you?"

"Yes, three. We have the second largest NICU in the city, after the university."

"Again, just for the record, are you being paid to be an expert witness for the defense?"

Newton objected to Jones's line of questioning.

"I think it's relevant," Jones said calmly. "Please instruct him to answer."

"We'll discuss it. Go ahead and answer," Newton instructed his expert witness.

"Yes."

"How much?"

"Objection."

"Same response," Jones said. "Please answer."

"I charge two hundred fifty dollars an hour for reviewing records and for giving depositions or testimony in court."

"If I may ask, why that rate?"

"You may. I'm not in the business of testifying. I limit the number of cases I look at, remembering that my primary job is in the NICU."

Kline squeezed Jones's arm, indicating he would take over. "Have you ever testified for the plaintiff?"

"I've never been asked."

"Are you familiar with the Smith case?"

"Yes."

"Were you involved in any way with the care of the baby?"

"No."

"So your familiarity with the case comes from record review?"

"Yes, and from discussions with Mr. Newton."

"Please tell us your opinion of what happened."

"This baby has a rather severe case of cerebral palsy and is almost certain to be severely retarded. The extent of damage is so great that the baby has never learned to suck and does not effectively swallow. For that reason, a gastrostomy was done and a tube placed through it in order to feed him and to allow him to go home. However, at home, the baby will need almost constant care."

"What is the prognosis for this baby?"

"It is unlikely that he will live for more than a year or so. Even with the feeding tube, it is almost certain that the baby will have fluid go back up his esophagus, like vomiting. When that happens, because he cannot swallow effectively, he will aspirate that fluid down into his lungs and develop pneumonia. He may survive one or two episodes, but that's all."

"That's a rather grim prognosis," Kline said sternly.

"Yes, it is. I hope the family has been told."

"What, in your opinion, is the cause of the CP in this baby?"

"It's hard to know for sure, but I am certain it did not originate during labor as alleged."

"Why is that?"

"The natural history of the disease is that ninety-five percent or more of these babies have an insult which causes CP during the sixth or seventh month of pregnancy. That's when the fetal brain is mature enough to survive the insult, whatever it is, but not mature enough to avoid being damaged. This is the primary reason fetal monitoring has not changed the incidence of CP at all."

"How do you explain the abnormal fetal heart-rate tracing?"

"I think that's relatively easy."

"If you don't mind, please tell us. I'm dying to hear."

Jones nudged him.

"I'm sure you are. I think the baby was abnormal from the start as evidenced by the lack of variability in the heart rate tracing from the time the monitor was put on. In other words, it was already too late. The drops in heart rate which occurred would not have happened if the baby's brain were not already severely damaged. I'm a little surprised, though, that there wasn't a trace of meconium in the amniotic fluid. The cesarean section did save the baby's life, but it did not, and could not, prevent the CP, no matter when it was done."

Kline asked several questions about meconium and then cut right to the heart of the matter.

"Are you telling us that Dr. Jankowski should not have done the cesarean section?"

"No, I am not. What I said was that the timing was unimportant in the sense that doing it earlier would not have helped. If it had been done much later, the baby would certainly have died. Another one of the problems with this disease, CP, is that we can't predict the severity of it until after the baby is born. In addition, there was some chance the baby could have been normal. The timing of the c-section was appropriate."

"You stated earlier that almost all cases of CP begin in the third trimester of pregnancy."

"That's correct."

"That means that a few cases begin in labor."

"That's also correct. Very few, and they usually have an easily recognizable cause, such as abruptio placentae, vasa previa, placenta previa, cord entrapment or entanglement, an anesthesia accident, or a traumatic delivery. None of those happened here."

"I must interrupt. Please define those terms."

"Abruptio placentae is the premature separation of the placenta, before the baby is born. Vasa previa occurs with placental blood vessels run through the membranes in front of the baby, where they can tear. Placenta previa means that the placenta is implanted over the opening in the cervix in front of the baby. Is that enough?"

"Yes. Go ahead, if you have more."

"As I said, none of those things happened here. In addition, when something goes wrong in labor at term, the baby is usually strong enough to survive with an intact, normal brain. Those where the brain is so severely insulted that it is damaged during labor have a terribly guarded outlook. They rarely survive the first year."

"Isn't that what you are predicting here? It seems to me that you have just described the Smith labor and baby."

"No, I haven't. No accident such as abruptio placentae took place. This case fits only the scenario I've described earlier."

"How can you be so certain?"

"Mr. Newton, may I introduce the CT results?"

Newton responded.

"Herb, Jefferson, I'm sorry. We just got this report early this morning. I really didn't mean to surprise you with it. I thought Dr. Thomas would call you. I guess he didn't."

"May we have a copy now?" Kline asked Newton.

"Yes, here it is. Go ahead, Dr. Dobbins."

"The CT scan shows a porencephalic cyst on each side of the brain. These occur only in the developing brain, very rarely at term. They take several weeks to develop. This means that something happened at the sixth or seventh month that caused spasm of the blood vessels to these areas so severe that the brain became ischemic, or blood and oxygen deprived. It infarcted, and the cysts are part of the healing process. This baby was irreversibly damaged well before labor and birth. Actually, I'm surprised he survived at all. If a CT had been done shortly after birth, these cysts would have been found, and that would have prevented any speculation about the CP occurring during labor."

"Needless to say, we are stunned," Kline said. "Can you speculate on the cause of the spasm and ischemia?"

"No, I can't at this point. I just learned about this today," Dobbins answered.

"I think we'll want time to think and consult about this. We may have to arrange another deposition from you, Dr. Dobbins. Do you have any questions, Jefferson?"

"No, that's all for now."

"Jefferson, that bastard, Thomas, may have done us in." Their trip back to the office was somber. "He didn't do a full workup on this baby, and then he didn't call me with the CT results. I wonder if he even bothered to look at them himself. I don't think we can do anything directly, but we sure can get out the word among the trial lawyers about this."

"I agree. That was a real shock this morning, and I don't think Clark was trying to sandbag us. As a matter of fact, I think that he was almost as surprised as we were. I don't think he and Dobbins had much of a chance to talk ahead of time. Now what?" Jones queried.

"If this CT business holds up, I think our only chance is Wilma James's testimony about the agony and turmoil the Smiths are going through. We'll use that to play on the sympathy of the jury. It looks like any chance of a settlement is gone. With a little luck, the judge will let us bring the baby into court. That's a sure tearjerker for the jury. Wilma James is scheduled tomorrow. That gives us this afternoon to prepare. I think we have to finish the deposition to justify all the money that the Smiths have spent on this." Kline parked the car, and they walked to the door.

"Absolutely. At least Wilma James should be pretty straightforward," Jones stated.

"Dr. Dobbins, that was a real bombshell." Newton was clearly exultant. "We're not supposed to do that to our opponents, although I sure did enjoy the look on their faces. However, I'm sure both of them recognized my surprise, too. Can you speculate, off the record, about the cause of the cysts?"

"They were either from a congenital defect, or Mrs. Smith ingested some toxic substance at six to seven months. From what I've read, they were pretty much a model couple who cleaned up their act, what little cleaning up it needed, for the pregnancy. They both deny anything out of line, so I guess the cysts have to be from a congenital defect," Dobbins explained.

"Fascinating," Newton commented.

"Either way, I think we can prove that there was no malpractice by Dr. Jankowski. She should be relieved. I just wish we could do something about Thomas and Segal. They're nothing but hired guns who follow orders for large incomes. To make things worse, Thomas should have had a CT done earlier on in the game." Dobbins obviously had some experience in the legal arena. "Actually, Kline should have asked for one soon after he got involved. He should have known that it's standard. This could have all been avoided."

"You're right, but we still can lose," Newton interjected.

"I don't see how." Dobbins seemed puzzled.

"Kline and Jones may have enough invested in this that they have to go ahead, especially with a jury trial. They have one more deposition scheduled, with the nurse who is staying with the

Smiths. She'll be a good witness to their turmoil and upset. And if the judge lets the baby in the courtroom, the jury may very well be swayed against us. It's still risky."

"Let me know when, and if, you need me again," Dobbins answered quietly.

"I will. Thanks very much. Good luck with your mother."

"Mike, guess what?" Janet burst in the door that evening, jittery with excitement and anxiety.

"Something good must have happened to have you so fired up."

"We got the CT scan back, and it shows brain damage, which had to occur at six or seven months of pregnancy. That lets me off the hook, even though we can't explain it right now. Things are definitely looking better. Let's keep our fingers crossed." She explained everything Newton had told her, still excited, but with an odd tone.

"That's wonderful, honey."

"Dr. Dobbins, the neonatologist at Seacroft Hospital, testified today. He was even stronger than Kim about the CP not coming from anything in labor and delivery. They couldn't get to him at all, according to Clark. Then he dropped the bomb on Kline, the CT scan. Clark tells me that even he was surprised. Anyway, Clark feels that he has now proved conclusively that I didn't do anything wrong."

"Janet, that's great news. Let's celebrate."

"Not yet, Mike. The bad part is that Clark says that Kline's going ahead with the deposition from Wilma James. He called me with that news late this afternoon. It's tomorrow."

"Why would he do that now?"

"Clark thinks it's to get her ready for a jury trial, where they'll use her as evidence for all the turmoil and disruption at the Smith house. That, plus the baby with a tube in its stomach, lying there in court, may be enough to get the judge and jury to find in their favor."

"Janet, that's not right. I can't believe the courts would allow that to happen."

"Mike, I didn't think so, either, but Clark is still worried, so I'm even more scared. It's been like a roller coaster today." She began to sob.

"Come on. Let's see some of the old Janet I used to know— tough as nails and not afraid of anything."

"Maybe that's it. I'm old. I know I don't feel tough, don't want to be tough, and don't want to do this ever again," she gulped out and caught her breath. "I don't even want to leave the house in the morning, let alone go to the hospital."

Mike sat on the arm of the chair next to her, holding and hugging her.

"Janet, it's almost over. Don't give up now, okay?"

"This is just so hard," she cried.

"I know, but we can't let these people beat us."

Her depression had seemed to level out, but the phone call about Wilma James's deposition put her back into the depths of despondency. She awoke that night imagining that she was back in her car in the garage, and she could actually smell the fumes. In her terror, she awakened Mike, who held her the rest of the night.

"Janet, we need to see a therapist," Mike said in the morning. "I don't think you can handle another night like last night. I know I can't. Please let me get appointments for this afternoon or tomorrow."

"I guess so. Go ahead. I can always cancel if I change my mind."

Mike called as soon as he reached his office and was able to get them in at one o'clock that afternoon. Both he and Janet arranged their schedules to be there.

21

"Mrs. James."

"Ms. James."

"I apologize. Ms. James, this is Clark Newton who represents Dr. Jankowski and Memorial Hospital. He will be doing most of the questioning today. Have you ever given a deposition before?" asked Kline. They were arranged around the marble conference table in Kline and Jones's office.

"No, I haven't. I'm a little nervous." She was perspiring.

"We understand," Kline told her. "The purpose of a deposition is to allow the opposing sides in a lawsuit to get an idea about what the strengths and weaknesses of the opposition's case are. It should be straightforward, and all the facts and truths of the case should be laid out by the time all the depositions are completed. From that, the opposing teams of attorneys may negotiate or go to trial. There will not be any attempt to intimidate you. However, the questions can be very pointed, forcing a precise answer, so that all concerned fully understand what is being said. Do you have any questions about the procedure?"

"What do I do if I need to go to the toilet?" Wilma looked frightened.

"Just say so. We can stop anytime," Kline reassured her.

She promptly seemed to relax, as if that were her only worry. "Thank you."

"Shall we begin?" Kline looked around the room.

"I'm ready," answered Newton.

"Do you swear to tell the truth, the whole truth, and nothing but the truth?" asked the court reporter.

"I do."

"Please state your full name," said Newton.

"Wilma Hunt James."

"I take it you're not married?"

"I'm divorced."

"How long have you been divorced?"

"Fifteen years."

"Are you a resident of St. Louis?"

"Yes, I've lived here all my life."

"You are a nurse, an RN, isn't that correct?"

"I am a registered nurse."

"Where did you go to nursing school?"

"I went to the two-year school at the city hospital before it closed."

"Have you worked as a nurse since then?"

"Yes, for thirty-two years."

"Was some of that in a hospital?"

"Yes, I worked at city hospital, in both obstetrics and in the nursery. That included labor and delivery, postpartum, and the newborn nursery." Wilma, who was dressed in her Sunday best, fidgeted, as always, but she appeared to be confident in her responses, and she was easy to understand.

"You're not doing that now?"

"No. That was about seven years ago. After twenty-five years, I switched to private duty nursing, usually in the home."

"What kinds of patients have you taken care of?"

"All kinds: people home from surgery, people with strokes or with cancer, and mothers and new babies. I like them best."

"How did you meet the Smiths?"

"Through the agency."

"What do you mean by the agency?"

"It's a home health care agency that hires nurses, aides, and the like. If you need help, you call the agency, and they try to fill your needs. The agency takes care of my salary, my benefits, and my insurance, and they send all the bills."

"When did you first meet the Smiths?"

"I met Mrs. Smith a couple of weeks before the baby was born, for just a few minutes. I didn't meet Mr. Smith until she came home from the hospital."

"Why just a few minutes? Getting to know each other seems relatively important in this type of situation."

"We scheduled an hour or so, but Mrs. Smith had a conflict."

"So, the first time you really got to know them was when they came home from the hospital?"

"That's right."

"What were they like when they came home?"

"They were pretty upset. She was crying. He really tried to help, but it didn't do any good."

"Why was she upset?"

"Wouldn't you be if your child had brain damage?"

"Certainly I would. However, I have to ask these questions so that anyone who reads the record the court reporter is typing will understand. Please bear with me."

"I'm sorry."

Newton stopped for a moment and poured her a glass of water.

"How have things been since Mrs. Smith came home?"

"I'd say they were pretty bad. She still cries all the time, and they yell at each other frequently. I don't think they're sleeping with each other even after all this time, at least that's what I hear them say. They never go out or do anything."

"Where's the baby now?"

"He came home several weeks ago."

"Can you tell me about the baby?"

"Sure. He's terrible."

"You'll need to explain."

"The baby has CP, and he's probably retarded. He just lies there, and hardly moves. He won't suck or swallow. He's got this tube in his stomach for feeding."

Newton asked a long series of questions about the details of the care of the baby.

"Is the baby growing okay?" he then asked.

"Yes, but barely. The doctors aren't happy with his weight gain."

"Do the Smiths take care of him?"

"No. He almost never even comes in the room, and she won't touch him. She comes in every day and just stands there and cries. It's horrible what's happened to these nice people."

"Are they both working?"

"Yes. He's been working since right after she came home. He used to come home late at night, which upset her. Then they argued."

"You said she's working, too?"

"Yes. She went back to work a few weeks ago. Now she's coming home late, too."

"You can't be doing all the care, twenty-four hours a day."

"No. There are two other nurses who come in nights and weekends now. I usually work the day shift. The baby needs almost constant care."

"So, you're not seeing so much of the Smith now that they're working and there are two other nurses?"

"I guess that's right. Remember, there's a cook and a maid, too."

Wilma asked for a bathroom break and was soon back.

"How can you be sure that they were happy before, that you're not seeing their normal dispositions right now? After all, you never really saw them before the baby was born, and you've really had only this time since the birth to observe."

"Believe me, this baby is so bad that no one, no matter who they are or how good they got along, could be normal after bringing that home."

"You didn't answer my question. How do you know that they were happy before, or are you just using woman's intuition?"

"The answer is, I've got my ways. Believe me, they've changed."

"Herb, what is going on?" Jones whispered.

"I don't know. She didn't say anything like this when we met yesterday. I guess we never asked her."

"I'm afraid you must answer better than that. How do you know?" Newton asked again.

"I just know.

"Ms. James, I think you're just guessing. If you have proof, we must hear it. If you don't answer, I can ask the judge to hold you in contempt."

Kline spoke up.

"Mr. Newton is being a little forceful, to which I object, but he is correct. You must answer."

"What's the question again?"

"You seem very certain that the Smiths have changed their behavior toward each other and toward the world in general. How do you know that, when you didn't meet them until after the baby was born?"

"I suppose this should remain confidential so I don't get into trouble, but after she went back to work, I started looking around the house. I stayed on the second floor though, so I could check the baby frequently."

"What happened?"

"Well, I found these videotapes of the two of them. That's how I know."

"Will you please describe the tapes? What do they show?"

"I found them in their bedroom along with a camera and tripod in a cabinet. They're tapes of the two of them. There's a TV and a VCR in there, too."

"When did you see this tape?"

"A couple of days ago."

"Is that the only time you looked at it?"

"Yes, but I won't ever forget it."

"So, it's fresh in your mind?"

"Absolutely."

"Herb, this could be a disaster," Jones whispered.

"Jefferson, think of something. We've got to stop this," Kline whispered back, holding his hand to his mouth.

"We can't, unfortunately," Jones said dejectedly.

"How do these tapes show you that their behavior has changed?" Newton continued.

"Well, remember when I said that I didn't think they were sleeping with each other now. Well, I know that's true because that's part of what they yell at each other about. The tapes show them in bed together when they were sleeping with each other."

"I take it that by sleeping together you mean having sexual intercourse?"

"Yes, but this was much more than that. They don't have anything on, and the covers are pulled down. It's obvious that they wanted everything to show on the tape."

"What were they doing?"

"Everything and anything. It's more than I've ever seen on cable TV. They were both enjoying all that stuff, laughing and carrying on. They certainly have changed."

"Were any of these acts during her pregnancy?"

"Objection," Kline yelled.

"I want to know if being pregnant caused a problem for them, if they started fighting then," Newton answered.

"Ms. James, did these tapes have dates on them?" Kline then asked.

"Yes. Dates and times."

"Okay, answer the question about pregnancy," Kline conceded.

"They sure were doing it during pregnancy. The last tape was when she was about six and a half months pregnant."

"What did they do?" Newton asked.

"They did everything. Some of the time, she was on top, and some of the time they did it with their mouths."

"Did she have an orgasm?"

"Is that a climax?"

"Objection," yelled Kline.

Newton explained, matter-of-factly.

"Orgasm can cause rather intense contractions, so the information given might be important to this case."

"Withdrawn. You may answer. Yes, orgasm is climax."

"She said she did, several times."

"You mean there was sound on the tapes?" asked Newton.

"Oh, boy, was there. I've never seen or heard anything like it. She said something like 'My God, this is fantastic.' "

"Did they do anything else?"

"Well, they were celebrating his new job and hers, which she was supposed to get when she went back to work after maternity leave, so they had some champagne."

"Anything else?"

"About halfway through the tape, they each sniffed some sort of white powder up their noses. He said he got it from someone at the office. I guessed it was cocaine or something like that."

"Are you certain of what you're telling us?"

"There's no way I could make up something like this. It's like nothing I've ever seen before."

"Where are the tapes now?"

"I put them back in the cabinet."

"Ms. James, are you absolutely certain of what you're testifying to?"

"Yes. The tapes are still there. You can look at them, too."

"No further questions. Thank you."

"Herb, Jefferson, I think this case is over," Newton said as soon as Wilma and the court reporter had left. "Cocaine is a known cause of ischemia of the brain of the fetus, especially at six to seven months. The alcohol and sex just make it worse. It looks to me as if the Smiths haven't told you or me the truth and that they are at fault rather than Dr. Jankowski. I don't think that either a judge or a jury will buy their story. Actually, it appears that they perjured themselves, whether or not they realize it. They should be reminded of that if necessary." He tried not to gloat.

"Clark, this is a bigger bombshell than the CT scan yesterday. Jefferson and I will talk about it, and we'll talk to the Smiths. I'll get back to you." Kline looked sick.

"Do what you have to do," said Newton.

"Jefferson," Kline said after Newton was gone, "if what Wilma James said is true, we're on a wild goose chase. I sure wish she had told us all of this when we first talked to her. I don't see any way of continuing with this case."

"I'm afraid you're right, but what if the Smiths destroy the tapes? That's easy to do, and then it would be their word against Wilma James, although swearing contests are unpredictable," Jones answered.

"I know, but Clark has heard Wilma testify. If the tapes should somehow get lost, I'm sure he'd insist on the Smiths being interviewed by an experienced counselor accustomed to working with drug abusers. I doubt they could stand up to that. It would come out sooner or later. Clark could even try to find the supplier at ZBL."

"You're right, Herb. I'm afraid the case is closed. And besides, we've heard the testimony, too. It would be unethical to allow any tampering with those tapes. When are you going to talk to the Smiths?"

"Right away. I'd planned for a meeting with them after this deposition anyway."

22

"Mrs. Smith, is Mr. Smith on the way?" asked Kline.

"Yes, he's parking the car. What's going on?"

"I think it's better if we wait until he's here."

"Oh, no. Has something gone wrong with the lawsuit?"

"Sorry I'm late," said Bill as he rushed in. "It was tough finding a place to park. What's going on?"

"I don't have an easy way to say this, so I'll be very direct," answered Kline. "Do you two take videotapes of yourselves in bed having intercourse?"

"I don't know what you're implying," yelled Angie, "but I don't like it."

"Those tapes are private. If anyone has seen them, they are guilty of breaking and entering," Bill growled.

"So, there are tapes. The person who saw them is Wilma James, who has the run of your house. While it may be somewhat unethical, I don't think you can make a criminal case out of it." Kline became stern. "More importantly, she watched a timed and dated tape of the two of you, when you were about six and a half months pregnant, Mrs. Smith. You were having sexual intercourse, and both of you were drinking something from a champagne bottle and sniffing a white powder into your noses. No jury in the world is likely to believe that it wasn't alcohol and cocaine. In addition you said you had rather intense multiple orgasms, Mrs. Smith, which do slow down blood flow to the uterus. That amount of alcohol and the orgasms alone probably would not have had any effect. However, in combination with cocaine, they are and were deadly."

The Smiths were ashen.

"If you'll remember what I told you about the CT scan yesterday, there are cysts in the baby's brain which are longstanding. We couldn't explain them, and we were going to use Wilma's testimony to get around them. Well, now we can't. They are almost certainly the result of a spasm of blood vessels in the baby's brain from the cocaine, causing too little blood flow, or ischemia, and resulting in infarction of the brain, like a stroke. The cerebral palsy and retardation were caused by your celebration. I must advise you that there are no grounds for a lawsuit." Kline sat back and folded his hands.

The Smiths sat totally silent for several minutes, stunned. Then Angie turned to Bill and snarled.

"Bill, damn you, this is all your fault. You brought that stuff home." The enormity of what she had said and done appeared to overwhelm her, and she slumped over and huddled in her chair, totally silent and unresponsive.

Bill moved over to hold her.

"The tapes are accurate," he slowly said. "It did happen as you describe. Neither of us thought of or realized the consequences. Oh, my God." Bill was pale and clearly shaken.

"Will you two be okay?" Kline asked.

"I don't know. This is more than I can take right now." Tears began to run from the corners of Bill's eyes. "I've been seeing a counselor. I'll do whatever is necessary to take care of Angie and Will. I hope Angie will be okay," he sobbed. "She hasn't handled this as well as I have and doesn't realize that she needs help." Bill slowly led Angie out, holding her closely.

"Herb, I don't think we should be paying Thomas and Segal the big fees they're demanding. In fact, we shouldn't pay them anything, unless we have to, or we should reduce the fee to the level Dobbins described and dare them to come after us. I don't think they will. I've been doing some figuring, and that should leave us about enough to cover our expenses. That way, we don't need to bill the Smiths for any more. They've got enough trouble right now."

"Jefferson, I think you're right. I'll call Clark and then those two. I think their days as experts are over. We'll have to be more careful in the future if we take a bad baby case again."

Kline telephoned Newton.

"Clark, the suit will be withdrawn as soon as I can get the paperwork done. The Smiths admitted that Wilma James was right. Off the record, we'll jab at Thomas and Segal a little, and maybe they'll quietly fold their tents. Sorry for the stress we caused, but we didn't know," Kline apologized, trying to make amends.

"I understand. Thanks for calling, Herb."

"Janet, this is Clark. The lawsuit's been dropped. We're all off the hook."

"Thank God. What happened?"

Newton explained.

Janet collapsed in her office chair, overcome with relief. She called Nancy to tell her the news, and then she phoned Mike.

"Mike," she sobbed happily, "it's over. We won."

"That's wonderful, Janet. Tell me all about it."

Janet quickly told him the story, hurried through her remaining patients, raced through rounds, and went home. As she drove, she felt as light as a feather. She could not wait to hug Mike and the children. They were waiting for her, and they clutched each other, tears of happiness streaming down their faces. After a short, but happy call to her parents, they all went to Garibaldi's to celebrate. Vince noticed the change in attitude and joined them by serving up extra spumoni for all.